Jonah and the Bitter Blues:
A Biblical Solution for Bitterness

JONAH
& the
Bitter Blues

A Biblical Solution
for Bitterness

by
Dr. John E. Neihof, Jr.

TELEIOS PRESS

Teleios Press

Copyright © 2017 John Neihof, Jackson, MS

Printed in the United States of America

First edition 2017

Cover design and book layout by Two Cups Creative

Cover Photo: © Can Stock Photo / mkm3

Printed in the United States of America

To all who have ever forgiven me for my failures.

To my wife, Beth, whose overflow of forgiveness shows
God's love and mercy to me.

Contents

Jonah 4

But it displeased Jonah exceedingly, and he became angry. So he prayed to the LORD, and said, "Ah, LORD, was not this what I said when I was still in my country? Therefore I fled previously to Tarshish; for I know that You are a gracious and merciful God, slow to anger and abundant in lovingkindness, One who relents from doing harm. Therefore now, O LORD, please take my life from me, for it is better for me to die than to live!" Then the LORD said, "Is it right for you to be angry?"

So Jonah went out of the city and sat on the east side of the city. There he made himself a shelter and sat under it in the shade, till he might see what would become of the city. And the LORD God prepared a plant and made it come up over Jonah, that it might be shade for his head to deliver him from his misery. So Jonah was very grateful for the plant.

But as morning dawned the next day God prepared a worm, and it so damaged the plant that it withered. And it happened, when the sun arose, that God prepared a vehement east wind; and the sun beat on Jonah's head, so that he grew faint. Then he wished death for himself, and said, "It is better for me to die than to live." Then God said to Jonah, "Is it right for you to be angry about the plant?" And he said, "It is right for me to be angry, even to death!"

But the LORD said, "You have had pity on the plant for which you have not labored, nor made it grow, which came up in a night and perished in a night. And should I not pity Nineveh, that great city, in which are more than one hundred and twenty thousand persons who cannot discern between their right hand and their left—and much livestock?" (NKJV)

Chapter 1

The Secret Sin of the Church

As our children were growing up, my wife and I enjoyed vacations with them. We saved our money all year long for two weeks of family togetherness, travel, and scenic wonder. We particularly enjoyed trips to the Rocky Mountain States and the national parks that grace them. One of our favorite stops was Yellowstone National Park in Northwest Wyoming. Yellowstone is known for its thermal features. Old Faithful geyser is remarkable in the regularity of its eruptions; every 70 to 90 minutes you can count on her!

The park rangers explained these unique features of Yellowstone to us. Certain variables must be in place: water, an underground plumbing system with constriction, and heat. The geography of Yellowstone uniquely blends these variables together, creating contrasting thermal characteristics.

The super-heated water of a geyser will build pressure in the plumbing system of the earth until it erupts with a powerful spew of heat, gas, and water. If the plumbing system is not constricted, the water may become a bubbling hot spring. Then there are fumaroles that can spew steam continuously, while others spew periodically.

I have concluded that pent-up bitterness expresses itself like the thermal features of Yellowstone National Park: geysers, hot springs, fumaroles. We may vent, boil, or spew our bitterness. Home, work, church, rush hour traffic, the grocery store... no area of life remains untouched from the debilitating and destructive force of bitterness.

Ministry often takes me to a variety of churches. Across the years of travel and itinerant ministry, I have observed that bitterness is the secret sin of the church that is frequently coddled, defended, spiritualized, and ignored, as it lurks in the pew, parish, and parsonage.

I know my darkest temptations. I know my most intense spiritual battles. Temptations to bitterness, often refused, sometimes embraced, have been among my most troubling passion. It is helpful to know about the cycle of bitterness to help understand and address it through the power of Christ.

Throughout my life, I have found myself grappling with my rights. Western civilization has conditioned us this way. We have been condition to insist upon our rights. We make sure that no one violates our personal autonomy, self-determination, and freedom of choice. We have our rights, and we aren't afraid to demand them!

But what about our expectations, the first cousin to our rights?

Each of us has expectations. We expect our elected leaders to perform their duties appropriately. We expect our spouse to remain faithful. We expect our children to obey. We expect the direct deposit of our paycheck to be in our account on payday. We expect other drivers to obey the rules of the road. We expect our waitress to serve our party first at the table in the restaurant. We expect our hot food to be hot, and cold food to be cold. We have expectations. What happens when our expectations are unmet?

Let's be honest. All too often, we are frustrated when we have to wait too long at the doctor's office. We are frustrated when the children don't make their beds. We are frustrated when our teenagers leave their belongings scattered like so many seeds throughout the freshly plowed field of our home. We are frustrated when teammates at work fail to complete their assigned duties, leaving the rest of the team hanging. All too often, we are chronically frustrated by unmet expectations.

Frustrated with others' failures to meet our expectations, we journey into the hearts, minds, motivations, and character flaws of others.

"She failed me because she is lazy!"

"He failed me because he doesn't like me."

We assign ignoble intentions to people who frustrate us. We construe them as out to get us, getting back at us, disliking us. We analyze, psychoanalyze, and attribute motives to each other; and we are especially good at identifying the deepest, darkest, most disgusting impulses... in someone else!

By the time we have traveled the path of demanding our rights, expecting others to meet them, experiencing frustration, and questioning motives, we are often seething with anger. "I'm so angry, I could . . ." And we stay on that path.

Sadly, many of us have spent so much energy generating anger, it seems to be the only emotion we know how to express. We have stretched our feeling vocabulary for anger to the breaking point, ignoring, and sometimes crowding out, other, healthier emotional expressions in our lives.

This is the overview of the emotional cycle that generates bitterness. Bitterness may bring us to a place of frustration and anger where we find ourselves saying, "I just want to quit!"

We may blame everyone else for the failure and frustration that has consumed us and destroyed our relationships and productivity. Clinging to our rights, insisting upon our own unrealistic expectations, developing frustration, and assigning motives to others will work us into a frustration with life that can overwhelm our emotional health.

The pages of this book will challenge you. If you are prayerful, God will examine you. He will probe your motives, expose your double-mindedness, and call you to holiness. He will convict you of those broken, bitter relationships in your life and call you to holiness and peace. He will love you until you bear His likeness. He will free your surrendered heart from bitterness and empower you to live in the fullness of His Holy Spirit.

Embrace the journey. You are not alone.

Chapter 2

Jonah— A Prejudiced Prophet

Some of us are living there today—amidst a frenzy of anger and bitterness. Some of us will openly express our bitterness with hostility, venting like a fumarole. Others will be like a hot spring, simmering quietly, suffering from a self-inflicted agony. Our geyser-like passive-aggressive response will reserve their emotional and verbal eruption until the moment of maximum devastation to ourselves and our relationships.

Are you on the path of bitterness? Some of us have dabbled with initial exploration. Others have traced the entire path. Still others have traveled the road of bitterness so often that they live a chronic lifestyle afflicted by the disability it brings.

The beauty of the journey is this: God longs to be with us. He walks with us, convicting, guiding, and transforming all along the way.

Enter the prophet Jonah! God was with Jonah even in the midst of Jonah's rankest and most repugnant attitudes. God was shaping and changing the prophet at every turn. He had to address the entirety of Jonah's person: his inner attitudes, his external relationships, and his relationship with Himself.

God wants to journey with you and me as well. Our bitterness offends Him. It prevents the intimacy of relationship He longs to enjoy with us. Our bitterness is an affront to His holiness, but He does not dispose of us. He addresses our bitterness. At times, He slowly peels back layers, gently moving us to wholeness. At other times, He seems to expose us entirely, demanding our immediate cooperation with His Lordship.

Occasionally, He even prepares a great fish of isolation and despair to cure us of our obstinate rebellion. He may seat us under a temporary gourd of protection, only to rip it away when our dependence moves from God to the gourd. All the while, He is drawing us to share in His character, His holiness. If He is to accomplish His goal, He must shape us to become like Himself. Holy. Loving. Clean from bitterness.

In some seasons of our lives, God's curriculum addresses our interior world. Some circumstances of life school us in the Divine discipline of relationships with others. Each of these experiences can be redeemed by God to cultivate godliness and Christ-likeness in us, so that deep, intimate fellowship with our Creator God becomes the sustaining life force of our existence.

I remember the story of Jonah from my earliest years. As a child I was fascinated with the series of events that led to Jonah being swallowed by the divinely-prepared great fish.

He was a prophet of God to the Israelites in the ninth century B.C. For generations, the Hebrew people had lived in the divided kingdoms of Israel in the north and Judah in the south. The violent Assyrians, just north of Israel, were threatening destruction and attacks upon their neighbors in a quest for world domination.

God called Jonah to serve as a missionary to evangelize the people of Assyria. All of his life, Jonah had been taught social, ethnic, and religious hatred of everything that the Assyrians represented. Jonah despised the paganism, the practices, and the people of Assyria. Nineveh, the Assyrian capital, was the hub of that vile culture.

Assyrian military assaults, for which they were the best known and feared, were terrifying. Their military tactics were innovative and violent; their methods of warfare were renowned in the early first millennium B.C. Mounted cavalry, chariots, battering devices, archers, and conquest characterized Assyrian warfare. Assyrians developed a style of attack where a hailstorm of arrows was fired from the bows of hundreds and thousands of archers. These arrows could be shot distances of 250 to 600 yards. The archers entered warfare armed to the hilt. The army even traveled with a manufacturing plant to make more arrows.

Worse, once they had conquered an enemy, the Assyrians were known for the most hideous forms of maltreatment of their surviving foes, atrocities which were legendary throughout the ancient world. The Assyrians recorded their military cruelties in murals that have continued to be studied by archaeologists. Stabbings, stakings, beheadings, and physical dismemberings were common methods of military terror and control of a people. Assyrian mutilators cut off hands, feet, tongues, and gouged out eyes of the conquered.

It was common to slash the bodies of the conquered open until their entrails spilled, and the mortally injured died a slow and agonizing death. The Assyrians would frequently slash open the belly of a pregnant woman, rip the fetus from her womb, and violently destroy the baby in the presence of the mortally wounded mother.

The Assyrians practiced flaying. The vanquished foe was fastened to a pole. The executioner then skinned him by making a skilled cut at the top of the back, loosening a flap of skin at the shoulders, taking hold of the flap of skin and peeling the skin of the victim from top to bottom. The Assyrians literally skinned people alive.

Staking was a form of Assyrian execution whereby the executioner skewered the condemned criminal with a lubricated stake inserted through the anus and into the abdominal and thoracic cavity, pushing aside internal organs, and pinning the condemned to the ground. Death often took days.

There was nothing humane about the Assyrians' military conquest or their version of law enforcement. They were human butchers.

Jonah also loathed the prospect that the God he worshiped, feared, and served, might demonstrate any mercy whatsoever toward the hated Assyrians. It was unthinkable to the prophet that a God of justice and judgment would mete out any mercy to this vile race! Jonah recoiled at the prospect that a God who expelled a sinful Adam and Eve from the Garden of Eden for their sin would show mercy to Nineveh. Jonah reckoned that a God who would mark a murderous Cain for his sin should never extend the hope of salvation to Assyria. He was certain that the God who destroyed the earth's population with a worldwide flood, saving only Noah and his family, would pound the gavel of judgment upon the Assyrians. It was unfathomable that a God who destroyed a lecherous, murderous Sodom and Gomorrah with fire and brimstone would do anything less toward Nineveh and its people. Mercy, grace, and salvation for Assyria and its people were incomprehensible to Jonah.

Even more nauseating than the salvation of Nineveh, was that Jonah might have any part in it. He hated Assyrians. They were evil. In Jonah's mind, they had zero redemptive worth, and Jonah thought he was justified in his hatred. No one, not even God, had the right to question his assumptions. He was not prejudiced. He was just right!

Or so Jonah thought.

He wanted to see the Assyrians destroyed. Jonah wanted judgment, and he was not alone. Although Jonah saw no hope for the Assyrians, he was afraid. Jonah most feared that the God of hope found hope for a hopeless nation. Jonah feared grace. He feared mercy. Jonah was mortified that God might extend both to the Assyrians when clearly the Assyrians deserved neither. Jonah would see to it that his version of justice was done, even if God would not!

He ran. Jonah ran to the Israelite port city of Joppa, the modern-day city of Haifa, Israel. There he boarded a ship headed for Tarshish. Nineveh was 500 miles northeast of Israel. Tarshish was over 2500 miles west.

Tarshish, Spain, on the shores of the Straits of Gibraltar, was the furthermost point from Jonah's homeland that he could imagine. He wanted to put as much distance between himself and the hated Assyrians as he possibly could. He wanted to outrun

God. If he could outrun God, he might outrun his call! If Jonah could outrun his call, he might outrun the possibility of any Assyrians being saved from God's just destruction of them. If he could outrun God, he might prevent God's misguided plan of salvation for the unregenerate Ninevites. If he could outrun God, Jonah thought he could ensure the damnation of an entire hated race of people. In his mind, that would be justice!

The ship to Tarshish, Spain, was consolation to Jonah. He slept a sweet peace of escape. But God was about to give Jonah an alarming wake-up call! The Mediterranean was rocked by a storm that caused the hearts of veteran sailors to quake with fear. The international crew called on various gods in assorted languages. The superstitious sailors resorted to an ancient method of discernment—casting lots. But the God of the storm asserted control of the lots.

Where was that Hebrew prophet? The captain found him asleep in the hold. The captain prodded the unrepentant prophet to his senses, and the lots were cast.

The lot fell on Jonah.

The moment of truth had arrived. Jonah faced the interrogation of an angry group of superstitious sailors. His presence was proving deadly to their pagan lives.

"Who are you?"

"Where are you from?"

"Who is your god?"

"What is your occupation?"

"Why is your god angry?"

"What do you think you are doing?"

The inquisition was earnest. The sailors' lives depended upon it!

The prophet's truth tumbled out amid the tempestuous sea-rocked ship. In a moment, the sailors knew that the Hebrew prophet was fleeing from his God. They did not know why, but they were certain about the reality that Jonah was on the run! Now, what to do about it?

Jonah, acting in a moment of uncharacteristic charity, sacrificed himself to the sea for the salvation of the ship and sailors. The sea calmed. The Divinely-prepared fish swallowed the prophet. The sailors praised Jonah's God.

The shouts of the sailors' praise on the ship never reached Jonah's ears. The water engulfed him the moment he hit the sea. The water pressure squeezed his chest. A fiery sensation burned within his lungs. His oxygen was nearly consumed. Darkness.

Jonah never knew how long he had lost consciousness. When he awoke, every sound, smell and touch was strange. Jonah saw nothing. Only darkness. The unfamiliar surroundings were indecipherable. Jonah thought he was in Hell.

In the darkness of the God-prepared inner sanctum of the fish, Jonah was brought face to face with his biggest problem—himself. He prayed! O, how the fleeing prophet prayed!

> *"I cried out to the Lord because of my affliction, And He answered me. Out of the belly of Sheol I cried, And You heard my voice. For You cast me into the deep, Into the heart of the seas, And the floods surrounded me; All Your billows and Your waves passed over me.*
>
> *"Then I said, 'I have been cast out of Your sight; Yet I will look again toward Your holy temple.' The waters surrounded me, even to my soul; The deep closed around me; Weeds were wrapped around my head. I went down to the moorings of the mountains;*
>
> *"The earth with its bars closed behind me forever; Yet You have brought up my life from the pit, O Lord, my God.*
>
> *"When my soul fainted within me, I remembered the Lord; And my prayer went up to You, into Your holy temple. Those who regard worthless idols forsake their own Mercy. 9 But I will sacrifice to You with the voice of thanksgiving; I will pay what I have vowed. Salvation is of the Lord." (Jonah 2:2-8 NKJV)*

After three days and nights of God-focused prayer, the rebellious prophet relented. He begrudgingly yielded to God's unrelenting persuasive pressure. Then with a mighty heave of regurgitation, the God-prepared prayer room of a fish vomited Jonah onto the dry ground of Assyria.

But that was just the beginning!

The prophet still had a 300-400 mile walk to Nineveh. And once he arrived in Nineveh, Jonah realized that it would take three days just to walk the circumference of the city!

Throughout the Old Testament, the prophets from God foretold coming Divine judgment against Assyria. Isaiah, Jeremiah, Nahum, Zechariah, Zephaniah, and Hosea joined the chorus with Jonah in decrying Assyria's wickedness and proclaiming impending judgment.

But Jonah's sermons were different. For Jonah, it was all very personal. He abhorred the entire racial-ethnic group of Assyrians with a vile hatred whose venom could not be reversed. Jonah wanted judgment without mercy on the Assyrians, even if he had to manipulate God to perform his will.

Nineveh, a great walled city of 100,000 people, was located on the banks of the Tigris River in the Northern part of modern day Iraq and served as the capital city of butchery and terror.

Jonah despised Nineveh. The very thought of calling such a people to repentance contradicted every value that he construed about God. The thought of offering these butchers the hope of salvation smacked of the worst miscarriage of justice.

God was asking Jonah to own His call to be a missionary, evangelist, and prophet to Nineveh and its people. But Jonah wanted to preside as judge and jury over the Assyrians, going far beyond his God-given job description. Jonah was coveting God's job.

Jonah was not too excited about the preaching part of his call. He knew God had called. He answered. His sermon was a brief and blistering message of destruction. "God is going to destroy this city!" The more he preached it, the more Jonah appeared to enjoy himself. Jonah seemed to find a certain solace in proclaiming death and destruction to the Assyrian military masters of death.

Once he began, Jonah was filled with fearless bravado. He eagerly embraced a tone of glee at the prospect of the death and destruction of Assyria. No mercy! No grace! "God is going to destroy this city!"

There was no love lost between Jonah and the Assyrians. Obey God? Yes, albeit begrudgingly. Love these people? No.

Jonah's message of destruction spread like wildfire. "God is going to destroy this city!" The Ninevites took up the proclamation. "God is going to destroy this city!" They began repeating, embellishing, expanding, and entreating one another to repentance.

To Jonah's chagrin, he had started a revival among the people he hated most. Each Assyrian who adorned himself in sackcloth was another dagger in the heart of the disgruntled prophet. Each Ninevite who covered his body with ashes was further irritant in the mind of the reluctant Jonah. Each fasting penitent was a source of frustration and anger to the regretfully successful servant of the Lord.

Revival had come to Nineveh! Jonah watched as the Ninevites changed their opulent attire and clothed themselves in the rough cloth of grain sacks. He was astonished at the sight of men, women, and children kneeling by a cold fire. They reached their hands into the salt and pepper colored ash. Fistfuls of ash filtered through hair and beards, until the repentant citizens of Nineveh were each seated in a personal pile of ash. The cloudy covering was streaked by rivers of tears tracing trails of repentance down their cheeks.

God was pleased.

Jonah was angry.

It was as Jonah had feared. His worst suspicions had proven true. God is love. Even to the Assyrians. Revival was revolting to Jonah's sensibilities.

So he pouted. He raged! The gracious God he had fled had failed him. The merciful God he feared would let him down, had done exactly that. The patient God had shown mercy on the people the prophet hated most. The kind God had relented to the repentant Assyrians, and Jonah's reluctant obedience had made him complicit in God's plan of grace!

It was Jonah's worst nightmare come true.

"Kill me now!" the self-pitying prophet begged.

God feared for the prophet's life and protected him with a rapidly growing vine and gourd. Jonah became quickly attached to the gourd's shelter, where he retreated to its shade and resentfully studied the hated Assyrians.

Under the vine, Jonah considered his rights.

"I have the right to hate these Assyrians. After all, they are the most wicked, vile, vicious race of people ever to walk the earth! And besides that, I have the right to demand God to destroy the Ninevites! After all, I am the one who spent three days and nights in the belly of a great fish! I have earned the right to insist upon my way! And besides, that's faith, isn't it?"

Nestled against the shade of the gourd, Jonah sang his bitter blues. He considered his expectations of God.

"I expect God to love justice and hate evil. These Assyrians are evil. If God shows them love, He really isn't true to Himself, is He? How can He be truly God if He does not judge those people? I expect Him to do His job!"

Jonah voiced his expectations of the Assyrians.

"You can't trust these people. Their kind will always lie and deceive to get their way. Besides, the moment you trust them, they'll turn on you, rape your wife, flay you alive, or impale you! They are all that way! They will never change. Not even God can fix that kind of people."

Resting in his shadowed vantage place overlooking the city of Nineveh, Jonah considered his frustrations.

"You know, I am so frustrated. I didn't want to evangelize these people. I ran. I boarded the ship to Tarshish, Spain. I was headed to the end of the world. I went as far as I could go to get away from this task. Even when I was thrown into the sea, I didn't want to preach to these people. I only did it because I had to. Even when I finally preached to them, I tried to focus on hopeless judgment. I know about grace, but I am not about to extend it to their kind! They don't deserve it! I was afraid that God would relent and let these vicious lowlifes off the hook! I knew it would work out this way. I just knew it would backfire on me. I knew it!"

Jonah's attempt to assign motives to everyone from the Assyrians to God Himself, only fed his frustration. Masquerading as a 9th century B.C. psychoanalyst, Jonah critiqued the Assyrians' culture, violence, motivations, and communication style. By the time he finished his analysis, Jonah believed that he understood quite well why these God-forsaken people had no hope of salvation! Jonah even took a stab at attributing motive to God for saving the lost Ninevites. He attacked and questioned God's character and motivation until he worked himself into such a state of doubt that he was not sure if he really believed in the goodness of God.

Squatting in his shelter, Jonah nurtured his anger. The longer he pondered his rights, his expectations, his frustrations, his assessment of the Assyrians' motives, and God's misplaced mercy, the angrier he grew. The indignant prophet found himself in such a bitter, enraged, depressed state that death seemed the only way out.

"Kill me!" he shouted heavenward.

Then, his only saving grace, the sheltering vine and gourd, died of a Divinely-sent worm. This was it—the last straw. The final act of injustice! The outstanding disappointment of a holy God! Poised in anger, Jonah tightened his fist to shake it heavenward, when suddenly, he heard the voice of God thundering at him.

> *"Then God said to Jonah, 'Is it right for you to be angry about the plant?'*
>
> *"And he said, 'It is right for me to be angry, even to death!'*
>
> *But the Lord said, 'You have had pity on the plant for which you have not labored, nor made it grow, which came up in a night and perished in a night. And should I not pity Nineveh, that great city, in which are more than one hundred and twenty thousand persons who cannot discern between their right hand and their left—and much livestock?'" (Jonah 4:9-11 NKJV)*

That response left Jonah steamed. How dare God rebuke him! He was an Israelite. He was one of God's Chosen People. Besides all this, he was the prophet of God, and he had his rights!

The notion that he, a prophet of God, must degrade himself to associate in any way with a culture of atrocity and terror was repugnant to him. It really did require a Mediterranean storm, being thrown overboard, swallowed by a great fish, held in a three-day time-out, and vomited on dry ground for the prophet to accept, however reluctantly, a call from God to Nineveh! Jonah was a bitter prophet, and he sang his bitter blues.

Chapter 3

The Cycle of Bitterness

Jonah's cycle of bitterness is much the same as yours and mine. As you journey through this chapter, think about your life's road and how it compares to Jonah's. Consider personal rights to which you are clinging, your expectations of others, along with the corresponding frustrations, misplaced assessment of others' motives, and the resulting anger and bitterness.

Numerous streams of experience contribute to my understanding of this cycle of bitterness. Personal relationships, trials, temptations, victories, along with my own failures have shaped my thoughts. Conversations with colleagues granted further insight. Years of pastoral counseling with college students fostered additional understanding of some of the process of anger, bitterness, and recovery. Daily reading of the Holy Bible has initiated change as the Holy Spirit continues to shape and remake me.

I confess that I am not an objective student of Jonah. I empathize with him. I even have to admit that I think I understand him, to some degree. Temptations toward bitterness are some of the deepest and darkest journeys of my life. If I know my heart and the Witness of the Holy Spirit at all, I have an assurance that I am living in obedience to God's Word, walking in His light, obeying the checks of the Holy Spirit, and not currently harboring any bitterness. I thank God for His Witness.

Recently, I sat at a lunch table in a popular Southern eatery. The linen tablecloths were covered with a fresh layer of paper. After a lunch of Southern cooking, I shared with a friend and fellow minister some of my pondering and musings. A light of recognition and conviction, followed by hope, sparkled in his eyes as I disclosed the truths I have learned about bitterness. A tear formed in his eye and trickled down his cheek along the crease by his nose. He wiped tears away. In that moment, the Holy Spirit witnessed that this line of truth is a critical need of the church.

I shared my first public teaching of this truth from Jonah before an audience of seminarians, faculty, and staff. It was obvious that the message about bitterness and the believer hit a raw nerve.

As I mentioned in an earlier chapter, bitterness is the secret sin of the church. Many believers seem to only talk about their battles with bitterness in a sinful attempt to defend it and spread its venom. Surely, such a flawed approach to our pain and sin grieves our Lord Jesus Christ.

The story of Jonah is one marked with a series of unusual events. We remember the story of Jonah's running from God because God was calling him to preach to the hated Assyrians of Nineveh. We remember how Jonah was on a ship going the opposite direction from where God was calling him. We remember how the ship was tossed about in the storm. We remember Jonah's being thrown overboard. We have even joked with one another, saying, "You must be the Jonah in our midst!"

We remember the story of the great fish that God prepared. We remember the story of the fish vomiting Jonah on dry ground on the shores of Assyria. A few of us may even remember Jonah's prophecy to the Ninevites. We remember the great revival that astonished Jonah and made him utterly angry against God for his mercy to the hated Assyrians.

But very few of us ever talk about Jonah chapter four; we forget the story of the gourd. However, I want you to think about Jonah's gourd. I want you to think about Jonah's problem with God's mercy toward the Assyrians. I suggest that the problem which Jonah faced in chapter four was a problem of bitterness.

In Jonah, and in us, bitterness produces a destructive and dysfunctional loss. Bitterness drains our productivity, ambition, energy and optimism. Bitterness is caused by a spiritual process of clinging to personal rights, demanding one's own expectations to be fulfilled, accompanying frustration, unwholesome assessments of others' motives, and anger.

Let us review the story of the prophet Jonah's bitterness.

> *"But it displeased Jonah exceedingly, and he became angry. So he prayed to the LORD, and said, 'Ah, LORD, was not this what I said when I was still in my country? Therefore I fled previously to Tarshish; for I know that You are a gracious and merciful God, slow to anger and abundant in loving kindness, One who relents from doing harm.*
>
> *"'Therefore now, O LORD, please take my life from me, for it is better for me to die than to live!' Then the LORD said, 'Is it right for you to be angry?'*
>
> *"So Jonah went out of the city and sat on the east side of the city. There he made himself a shelter and sat under it in the shade, till he might see what would become of the city.*

And the LORD God prepared a plant and made it come up over Jonah, that it might be shade for his head to deliver him from his misery. So Jonah was very grateful for the plant. But as morning dawned the next day God prepared a worm, and it so damaged the plant that it withered. And it happened, when the sun arose, that God prepared a vehement east wind; and the sun beat on Jonah's head, so that he grew faint. Then he wished death for himself, and said, 'It is better for me to die than to live.' Then God said to Jonah, 'Is it right for you to be angry about the plant?' And he said, 'It is right for me to be angry, even to death!'

"But the LORD said, 'You have had pity on the plant for which you have not labored, nor made it grow, which came up in a night and perished in a night. And should I not pity Nineveh, that great city, in which are more than one hundred and twenty thousand persons who cannot discern between their right hand and their left-and much livestock?'"

(Jonah 4:1-11 NKJV)

THE END!

Do you find yourself astonished by the way the Book of Jonah ends? It concludes with Jonah's rage against God and Nineveh and the prophet's death wish! God's rebuke punctuates the end of the prophecy. No apparent resolution. No epilogue. No record of the events of Jonah's life after Jonah 4:11.

Clinging to Personal Rights

As I think about this fourth chapter, I see a picture of the prophet Jonah clinging to his rights. Jonah has already demonstrated that he had some distorted, prejudiced notions about the Assyrians. Then he punctuates his disgruntled attitude with an implied response which insists, "I have a right to feel the way I feel!"

Jonah obviously was not about to release or relinquish his feelings or his judgments against the Assyrians. "After all," Jonah seems to say, "these Ninevites here in the capital city of Assyria are the most brutal military force in the world. They conquer people and then they brutalize them with the most heinous kinds of war crimes imaginable. They commit Holocaust against their vanquished foes. The ones they don't brutally exterminate, they enslave. I have the right to have expectations of God! I have the right to expect God to judge these Assyrians! And He'd better not show these animals mercy!"

Bound by Expectations of Others

Jonah was bound by expectations. He had demanding expectations of other people and of God. These expectations fueled a deep and growing anger. Jonah demanded that God and others meet his expectations. He prejudged and judged the Assyrians.

He preferred that God would send fire to consume them, and he was angry at God for not meeting his demands.

Jonah did not take God's challenge toward his feelings well at all. When God confronted Jonah about his anger, Jonah angrily resisted God's challenge. Jonah's emotions spiraled destructively downward. The raging fury within him was stoked with the fuel of bitterness and anger.

God's confrontation was intended to offer Jonah hope, wholeness, and healing. Jonah's resistance to God rejected everything good that God was offering him.

Jonah gives us a powerful lesson. The problem of bitterness moves through the same process in both Jonah and in us. It is a process that started with Jonah clinging to his rights as a desperate attempt to seize control when life seemed to be out of control. Jonah insisted upon being in charge, upon his right to define life and ministry on his own terms. He demanded to define the terms of God's call. Jonah desperately defended his rights to everything he identified as his own.

Saint Paul reminds us that we are not our own:

> *"Or do you not know that your body is the temple of the Holy Spirit who is in you, whom you have from God, and you are not your own? For you were bought at a price; therefore glorify God in your body and in your spirit, which are God's." (I Corinthians 6:19-20 NKJV)*

God had a greater purpose for Jonah's body than even Jonah could imagine. God kept insisting that Jonah offer himself completely and entirely to His Lordship. Jonah responded by demanding control. His self-righteous, self-absorbed vision for his life was far too small for a God who loves the whole world.

Frustration and Anger

Like the bitter prophet, our unfulfilled expectations of others frustrate us and leave us angry. We cling to our rights. We want control of our own lives. We want to control our children. We want to control others. Our fearful demands to control effectively squeeze the very joy out of life and relationships that God means to sustain us. Our inability to control each target of our ambition results in anger and frustration.

Such was Jonah's relationship with God. His demand to control God prevented the life of God from sustaining him. It was a futile attempt to cut God down to a size that Jonah thought he could manage. Jonah's inner bitterness corrupted his interpersonal relationships and distorted any hope of genuine intimacy with God. Simply put, his failure to succeed in his attempts to control God made Jonah mad.

In C.S. Lewis' *The Lion, the Witch, and the Wardrobe*, one of the children asks Mr. Beaver if the lion Aslan, the Christ figure of the narrative, is safe.

"Safe?" said Mr. Beaver; "Don't you hear what Mrs. Beaver tells you? Who said anything about safe? 'Course he isn't safe. But he's good. He's the King, I tell you."

Jonah's God is not safe, but He is good. Beyond Jonah's control? Yes. Good? Most certainly. But Jonah struggled to believe it. So he became angrier and angrier.

Americans identify with Jonah. What do Americans do with authority we cannot control? We throw them out of office! What do we do with pastors we cannot control? We fire them.

Early in marriage I learned something about control. I realized that all of my attempts to control my wife were futile! Every time I attempted to control her, I hindered and distanced the relationship between us. My controlling actions made my young wife angry. My failed attempts at control angered me as well.

The Lord Jesus brought me to a point in my marriage that I realized that I could not afford myself the luxury of attempting to control my wife, if I were to enjoy a Christ-centered marriage and home. Control kills relationships! I had to learn to love my wife. Loving her meant forgiving her even when she had done nothing wrong except to fail to fulfill some unspoken, petty expectation that I held. Loving my wife meant surrendering to God my right to control her.

The same lesson that applies to intimacy in marriage applies to the relationship between the Creator and the created. If I try to control God, I kill any relationship of intimacy that I hope to cultivate between us. It is only by surrendering to His Lordship my selfish ambition to control God that I begin to find true intimacy with my Creator.

Control kills relationships. Such was the sin of Jonah. Jonah was attempting to control a God that he desperately needed to sustain him. His angry attempts at control alienated the very Life Force that was intended to succor the prophet.

We repeatedly fight the battle of rights, expectations, control, and resulting frustration in our lives. We have expectations of people. We seek to preserve and defend our rights. We demand that our expectations be fulfilled. As long as you and I pursue this path, we chronically frustrate and anger ourselves.

When "I" seek to be the center of my universe, I will destroy myself. The same is true for you. The self-centeredness that was destroying Jonah is the same kind of self-centeredness that will destroy you and me. Jonah's sin of self-centeredness masqueraded as an attitude of self-determined social justice, a motive which God judged as entirely unjust and unacceptable. Jonah's attempt to legitimize unforgiveness and bitterness could not pass muster with an all-seeing, all-knowing God.

Assessments of Others

While rights feed expectations, and expectations feed frustrations, frustrations feed our assessment or appraisals of other people's motives. Attribution theory is an interesting concept from the fields of psychology and communication. Attribution theory suggests that people attempt to assign or attribute rationality and motivation to the words and actions of others. We seek to assess another person's motives to explain their words and actions. Then we label those motives with words.

Research findings from attribution theory indicate that people who are better at identifying and appraising the conversational motives of another tend to be better communicators. That is to say, people who are better at accurately identifying others' rationale and motivations are able to respond more accurately and intelligently to them in informed conversation.

I am a fairly competent communicator and make reasonably accurate assessments of what others are seeking to accomplish in conversation. I have honed a set of perceptual skills whereby I can read another person fairly well, interpret a message, and then adapt subsequent messages to that person in such a way as to construct shared meaning in a reasonably competent interaction.

But my skill has a dark side.

Sometimes I find myself explaining the words and actions of another in a way that projects my perceptions of character, personality, thoughts and motives upon the other person. As you know, our initial perceptions of another are not always accurate. The more I dislike another person, the darker my judgmental tendencies become.

I can quickly assess or appraise another person's motives in a way that deteriorates into the judging of that person's motives. The thought process goes something like this.

"I didn't like what he said." "He said that to hurt me!"

"What have I done to offend him?"

"He doesn't like me."

"He is out to get me."

"I must defend myself."

This subjective thought process of assigning ignoble motives to another and promptly judging them as matching my bias against them is precisely the kind of judging Jesus forbids in Scripture.

"Judge not, that you be not judged. For with what judgment you judge, you will be judged; and with the measure you use, it will be measured back to you. And why do you look at the speck in your brother's eye, but do not consider the plank in your own eye? Or how can you say to your brother, 'Let me remove the speck from your eye'; and look, a plank is in your own eye? Hypocrite! First remove the plank from your own eye, and then you will see clearly to remove the speck from your brother's eye." (Matthew 7:1-5 NKJV)

My appraisal skills can serve me well in human interaction, or they can serve me poorly. I can use my skills to communicate more effectively, or to cultivate the poisonous fruits of defensiveness and hostility. When I pretend to be a psychologist, analyze another I construe as my enemy, and judge their motives as ignoble, I sin. Falling into this trap is poison to the spirit. It provides an unfair representation of another. This pattern of judging another is devoid of grace, mercy, and kindness. Such a pattern always leads to anger.

A word of caution must be exercised here. Our culture continually embraces the "judge not" dictum as a call to moral relativism. Christians often fall prey to such a distortion of truth. The judging which Jesus condemns is that of consigning someone to a lost eternal destiny. It is the moral and judicial equivalent of decreeing another to "go to Hell." Such judgment does not belong to human beings. Eternal damnation is a decision made by God alone.

However, certain judgments must be made by human beings or else life takes on an absurdity of impossible proportion. Teachers must grade papers. A defensive student dare not cry out, "Judge not!" Parents must discipline children. A self-preserving toddler dare not say, "Judge not!" to her father!

Authority is woven by God into the fabric of Creation. Authority must judge. But authority must judge behavior. The motivation of another is not generally ours to know.

"But the Lord said to Samuel, 'Do not look at his appearance or at his physical stature, because I have refused him. For the Lord does not see as man sees; for man looks at the outward appearance, but the Lord looks at the heart.'" (I Samuel 16:7 NKJV)

God has given humans the ability to judge behavior. Without proper exercise of this gift, life reaches an absurdity that reduces it to chaos. However, God has retained for Himself the ability to examine and judge human thoughts, hearts, and motivations. We dare not covet His job or assert claims toward that which alone belongs to God.

All too often, we have traveled a spiritual and emotional freeway of judgment, only to be arrested by the Holy Spirit when we realize that the road has led us down a super-highway of anger and bitterness. I see pastors who have traveled a road paved by rights and expectations, only to embrace a loathsome sort of anger while masquerading as a shepherd to the flock of God. I have seen church members embrace this thoroughfare of rights and expectations, only to fuel a kind of abusive hostility while they masquerade as Christian. Such is counterfeit to the Gospel of Jesus Christ.

I spent twenty-three happy and productive years as a Bible college professor and administrator. I was 29 years old when I joined the faculty as a part-time instructor. It was my first full-time, career track position. I was young, idealistic, ambitious, and gifted. Words came quickly to me. Not all of them were adequately thought through! Too often, I reacted out of my inability to properly manage my emotions.

As a child, I remember a saying my father printed out with a plastic label maker and stuck to the fluorescent lamp above his desk. It read: "Be sure your brain is engaged before putting your mouth into gear."

Three years into my career, I joined forces with a new, vigorous president at the college. Expectations were high. Work abounded. Success was achieved in many endeavors. When the President had an initiative he wanted to pursue, I positioned myself as his internal public relations assistant. He was reserved. I was quick to speak. I defended his positions. I sought to advance his agenda. In the process, I hurt some people. I caused some strained relationships. I tried to control too many things.

In my early years, I think I had some very flawed views of myself. I was the only full-time employee of the organization with a Ph.D. I had grown up in the organization. I understood its culture. Certainly, I had the right to speak on issues! I had the ability to see through complex problems quickly, to think on my feet and form the words necessary to defend and advance my position. But these gifts were a two-edged sword. On one occasion a colleague told me, "We know better than to back John into a corner. He will come out fighting."

That observation exposed my blind spot. There was a lot of truth in my colleague's statement. I had forgotten the important saying stuck on the lamp above my father's desk.

Over the years, the Holy Spirit has continued to refine my character. He faithfully and gradually revealed to me my false perceptions of myself. He revealed personal rights to which I was clinging, expectations of others that contributed to the frustration of living and working together in community, misplaced appraisals of others' motives, and tendencies to anger and bitterness. He allowed me to pursue just enough of my own misguided path that He could get my attention, arrest and redirect me.

I have worked with people who never successfully negotiated these troubled waters of rights and relationships. I have observed those who jump from job to job, employer to employer, address to address, marriage to marriage, and family to family, all because they could not accept God's discipline and correction to relinquish their rights and learn to live in right relationship with God and others.

I am certain that I, like Jonah, have further lessons in God's classroom of correction. I pray that the lessons I have learned will stand me in good stead for the next set of lessons to come. I pray the same for you.

As you consider and apply the concepts of this chapter, think about personal rights to which you are clinging, expectations you have of others, corresponding frustrations, misplaced assessments of others' motives, and the resulting anger and bitterness. Then, pursue a path of healing, wholeness, and holiness that is outlined in the upcoming chapters of this book.

Chapter 4

Funny Way to Love!

A large part of our spiritual development involves God's nurture. God seeks to nurture within us the virtues of emotional self-control and behavioral self-discipline. God was seeking to cultivate these virtues in Jonah, and He used Divine discipline to effect the development of Jonah's character.

Experiencing discipline is an unsavory ordeal for most of us. We can accept notions of self-discipline, but externally imposed discipline is a bit more difficult for us to handle. Discipline cuts against the quest for autonomy and independence. Authority asserts discipline when we are wrong. We are embarrassed. We lose face. We don't like it.

Jonah seems to feel much the same way. I can almost hear Jonah crying out to God, "Don't tell me how I am supposed to feel about the Assyrians!"

God was trying to move Jonah into position so that Jonah could succeed. Jonah did not see it that way. Jonah felt controlled. He felt pushed into doing something that went against every thought and emotion he had toward Nineveh.

God disciplines those he loves.

We don't like to hear it.

We don't like to experience it.

But it is still true.

God was disciplining Jonah's thoughts, actions, motives, and emotions. He was seeking to bring Jonah to a place of spiritual and emotional health, while accomplishing His eternal purpose.

God's purpose is to save lost people. Jonah was okay with that as long as God's salvation reached worthy people whom Jonah liked. But when God's call to repentance and salvation ran cross grain with Jonah's world, Jonah resisted God's design.

God's purpose often runs cross grain to your emotional world, and to mine. That is when God must discipline us. His discipline is to bring our thoughts, emotions, and actions in line with His holy character and purpose. Why does the God of the universe take time to shape people like us toward His holy likeness? Because He loves us. He longs for relationship with us. Hence, he disciplines us that we may "share in His holiness," allowing intimacy and relationship between Creator and created.

Cooperation with God's discipline was a problem for Jonah. His lack of cooperation hindered intimacy with His Creator God. Jonah's bitterness against the Assyrians blinded him against God's larger purpose, the salvation of the lost. God had to discipline Jonah in a quest to correct Him.

I have a healthier understanding of God's loving correction because of the loving correction of my earthly father. John Eldon Neihof, Sr., is the holiest, godliest person I know. I admire my father and desire to emulate the goodness of character that God has grown in him. But God did not cultivate virtue in Dad without a cooperative subject. Dad lovingly cooperated with the journey of character transformation in a lifelong relationship with our Heavenly Father.

My father was always a good disciplinarian in our home. He disciplined with love and firmness. Dad explained to my brother and me how he had been disciplined. My Grandpa, Ernest Neihof, was self-employed in a garage that he operated and co-owned with Al Fender. He often worked long hours, and much of the discipline fell to Grandma Neihof. Grandma and Grandpa Neihof were loving parents, but they believed in what we now refer to as "corporal punishment." Dad explained it this way: "They applied the board of education to my seat of understanding. They believed in making an all-American boy out of me. They applied the stripes, and I saw the stars!"

On one occasion, Grandma felt it necessary to discipline my daddy. He was just a boy, her youngest child. As she prepared to apply the teaching tool to the teachable moment, Grandma told Dad, "I only do this because I love you."

My self-pitying father formed an unspoken retort in his mind, "Hmmph. Funny way to love!"

> *"For whom the LORD loves he corrects; even as a father the son in whom he delights."*
> *(Hebrews 12:6 NKJV)*

Once my father grew to adulthood and marriage, he and Mom soon became parents. They entered parenting with deep love and affection for us children. After a heartbreaking miscarriage, I was the firstborn. My brother, James, is twenty months younger. Marcia and I are eight years apart, and Mary and I, thirteen. Mom and Dad disciplined us lovingly, fairly, firmly, and consistently. Spankings were not a frequent option, but they were always an available one.

As boys, James and I really began to get into cracking bull whips. We both had them. Somewhere along the way, we had seen television or photos portraying a cattle drive. We were impressed by the talent and power of the head wrangler of the drive. He possessed the bull whip. My brother, James, soon became a master of the bull whip. He could not only crack it, but he could twirl it above his head and snap it in such a way that made that 6' bull whip resound with a powerful crack, as good as any firecracker.

One day when James and I were about eight or nine years old, one of us decided to take a bull whip to school. I think James was the one to bring it on this occasion, but I claimed that this particular bull whip belonged to me. It was the start of the school day, probably about 8:30 a.m. We had been to a chapel service for the Mount Carmel Elementary School. Upon dismissal from chapel, we were walking across the Mount Carmel campus. We were between the Administration Building and the Paulo home–our classroom was in the basement of that home–when I realized that my brother had MY bull whip.

I turned on James like an angry sow bear whose cub had just been stolen. You must understand that my younger brother has been larger than I since I was four years old. Blinded by rage, I knew no reason. He had taken my bull whip without my permission! Before he knew it, my sense of justice and judgment had knocked my larger foe to the sidewalk leading down to our elementary classroom in the Paulo basement. Caught in a mighty death grip, we rolled, punched, and pulled. I would retrieve my bull whip from his thieving grasp!

Unbeknownst to James and me, in the midst of our rolling and wrangling, the crowd of elementary onlookers gathered around us cheering on the fight. At the same time, the Mount Carmel High School chapel service had just dismissed. Dad always went to chapel. On his way from chapel to his classroom, he had to pass directly by us. Suddenly, two great hands parted the crowd. His powerful voice cut through the rabble, freezing us in each others' grasp. One hand grabbed James, and the other hand grabbed me. Before we knew it, we were on our feet. Taking hold of each of us firmly, Dad marched us thirty yards to the basement entrance of the elementary boys' bathroom through a side door of the Mount Carmel Library building.

Dad was aghast by our public display of rage. Very quickly, the bull whip was forgotten, and the more pressing issue of our anger and fighting was directly addressed. Within the privacy of that bathroom, he extended correction, in the form of spankings, to his sons.

Dad was a dorm supervisor at Mount Carmel, a boarding high school. Often, I watched my father correct one of the seventy boys in the boys' dorm. Never had I seen him lay a hand of correction on any of them. I had seen him lay a hand of comfort on them. I had seen him extend a touch of welcome to them. But no touch of correction. That was reserved for us, for we were his sons. And his touch of correction was firm and decisive!

> *"For whom the LORD loves he corrects; even as a father the son in whom he delights."*
> *(Hebrews 12:6 NKJV)*

The normal sequence of events leading to discipline went like this: infraction, observation, correction, warning, further infraction, discipline—in the form of a spanking with Dad's belt. Daddy then took us in his arms and assured us of his love for us. Prayer followed, and we were sent on our way with an admonition to behave ourselves.

James and I were familiar with the rod of correction. The rod was not used frequently, but when used, it was rarely forgettable. Between ourselves, never to his face, we referred to Dad as "Quick Draw." This reference out of the Old West highlighted the deftness with which he could unbuckle and draw the disciplinary tool of choice.

I was yet under the tender age of ten when I received my first Monopoly game as a Christmas gift. Oh, how I loved Monopoly! My brother and I soon learned how to play, and we would compete against each other zealously for hours upon end.

There is no other game quite like Monopoly. When you win, you win totally, victoriously, and mightily. And when you lose, you lose completely, devastatingly, and with great crushing humiliation. I played the game with a certain smug arrogance. This arrogance deeply annoyed my brother, James, especially when he was losing. He'd land on my hotel. I, having memorized the rental rates for each of the properties, would extend my hand and smugly pronounce his financial sentence! It galled him. I knew just how to irritate him, quietly prodding and provoking, until he blew up! It really wasn't intentional. It was just easy! Initially, Mom and Dad didn't realize the dynamics of my aggravation and James' explosion, and he, to my impish pleasure, would receive the force of the correction. As they saw my role in the provocation, I began to receive my fair share of correction.

One winter night, Dad played Monopoly with James and me. We were having quite a time of competition. I was about ten, and doing my general scheming, trading and building, always looking for an advantage. Twenty months younger, James didn't always see the strategy of my ways, but had been my victim enough times to have an appropriate suspicion as to my motives. I'd offer what he thought to be a sweet deal, then turn around and burn him with another high rent rate. It was great fun. I was smug. He was angry. My landlord exploitation of my brother continued as I sought to monopolize the board. Soon, James experienced the final devastating blow to his ego and prosperity. He landed on yet another of my growing properties. It was the last straw! The humiliating end! He knew it.

"You guys are a bunch of cheaters!" James erupted angrily. Then he ran to our bedroom, jumped to his top bunk berth, and under the covers.

Dad waited a moment, allowed me to conclude my victory, and then calmly pursued James to his berth in the top bunk. He would not allow one of his boys to have such an angry, out-of-control attitude. He would not permit his son to disrespect his paternal authority with a malicious accusation of cheating. That night, James received some strong discipline. A terrific spanking. Neither he nor I ever forgot it.

"For whom the LORD loves he corrects; even as a father the son in whom he delights."
(Hebrews 12:6 NKJV)

Perhaps it was that same year. We were on a family vacation going to Grandma and Grandpa's house. The car trip to West Virginia was always a long one for two boys. Dad was driving a 1969 Ford LTD. It was olive green with a black vinyl top. It had an eight-track tape player, our first car with such modern technology. The radio and eight-track player were left of the steering column. Marcia was in the baby car seat in the front.

James and I were sitting in the back seat on the slick, green, vinyl seats. You remember those kind of seats? When the vinyl seats were cool, you could slide back and forth on them like a playground slide. When they were warm, you'd get sweaty, and peeling your skin from the vinyl felt and sounded like pulling apart a Velcro strip!

We had just left home and were not even to Lee City, fifteen minutes into the four -to five-hour trek. James and I were at each other. Picking.

"Get off my side."

"Don't touch me."

"Don't touch my stuff."

Whiny. Irritable. Angry.

Dad corrected us verbally. "Boys."

More picking.

More correction.

It wasn't long before Dad had enough. He knew that it was a long trip and he'd better redirect the trajectory of his young sons' interactions, or it would escalate to a full-blown fight.

Suddenly, we heard the tires hit the gravel shoulder. The brakes pulled the '69 LTD to a stop. Dad put the automatic transmission into PARK. He opened his door and got out. He came around to the back door on the passenger side and beckoned James and me out of the car. He explained that we had a long car trip. He was not going to tolerate our whining and quarreling. He then spanked us both for our disobedience and put us back into the car.

We dried our tears as we were commanded, and traveled in silence. Now we were on the Mountain Parkway. Five, ten minutes passed. Tentatively, James and I looked at each other. We exchanged furtive grins. Soon we were whispering.

One of our elementary friends, Billy Watkins, had spoken a word of poetry or sung a few phrases of song that we remembered. It went, "In the shade of the old apple tree, my father..." and described the form of corporal punishment that had been administered. I suddenly remembered this song, and whispered some newly composed lines to my brother. We snickered.

Dad's ears perked up. "Boys, what's going on back there?"

My innocent response, "We just made up a song!"

Dad seem pleased with the sudden change in atmosphere.

"A song?" Ever a musician himself, he said, "Let's hear it."

I looked at James. He responded with a grin. We broke out in a duet: "In the shade of the old LTD, my daddy beat the tar out of me."

> *"For whom the LORD loves he corrects; even as a father the son in whom he delights."*
> *(Hebrews 12:6 NKJV)*

When we were Bible college students, James and I lived in our parents' home on the Bible college campus. During those years, James and I both met and courted girls whom we would later marry. James and his best friend, Tim, often hung out in our basement bedroom in our home at the college. Our girlfriends' pictures were openly displayed. I always knew when Tim had paid a visit, because he would do the same thing: he would take a marker and draw upon the glass on my girlfriend Beth's portrait. A mustache, a goatee, jewelry, objects coming out of her nose. He took any opportunity to graffiti my girlfriend's likeness. I tried to be patient, to go along, just clean it up, and be cool. But this time, I had enough. It had gone on for months. My brother knew about it and didn't defend me. It was time to stand up to all 6'4" of him and let him have it. I did.

It was loud. It was hateful. It was unkind.

Dad heard it.

He sat us down.

"What's going on?"

Dad allowed James and me to explain our positions. We both vented a belly full of anger at each other. Too much drama.

Then Dad let us know where he stood. No yelling. No spankings. We were 19 and 20 years old. But we knew the rule of the house: ZERO tolerance. We would get along. We would be kind. We would forgive. We would love each other. This atmosphere of anger would not persist. Not in his house. Apologies were made. Dad prayed with us, for us, and even preached at us in his prayer. Forgiveness. Dad had put down the law.

> *"For consider Him who endured such hostility from sinners against Himself, lest you become weary and discouraged in your souls. You have not yet resisted to bloodshed, striving against sin. And you have forgotten the exhortation which speaks to you as to sons:*
>
> *"My son, do not despise the chastening of the Lord, Nor be discouraged when you are rebuked by Him; for whom the Lord loves He chastens, And scourges every son whom He receives."*
>
> *"If you endure chastening, God deals with you as with sons; for what son is there whom a father does not chasten? But if you are without chastening, of which all have become partakers, then you are illegitimate and not sons.*
>
> *Furthermore, we have had human fathers who corrected us, and we paid them respect. Shall we not much more readily be in subjection to the Father of spirits and live? For they indeed for a few days chastened us as seemed best to them, but He for our profit, that we may be partakers of His holiness. Now no chastening seems to be joyful for the present, but painful; nevertheless, afterward it yields the peaceable fruit of righteousness to those who have been trained by it.*
>
> *"Therefore strengthen the hands which hang down, and the feeble knees, and make straight paths for your feet, so that what is lame may not be dislocated, but rather be healed." (Hebrews 12:3-13 NKJV)*

Are you feeling the discipline of your loving Heavenly Father? You may find yourself saying with my dad, "Hmmph. Funny way to love." Remember, it is God's way. I am amazed that God loves me enough to invest correction in my life. I am amazed that He sees me as a worthwhile investment!

Jonah was a slow learner when it came to understanding God's discipline. His close-mindedness to God's agenda proved a significant self-imposed disability to his own progress. Don't be a slow learner. Learn the lesson of our Heavenly Father's correction.

Perhaps you find yourself traveling a path strewn with rights, expectations, frustrations, appraisals, and anger. God, the Holy Spirit, has sought to discipline you along the path, yet you have resisted. Now you find yourself in full blown bitterness. God is lovingly orchestrating disciplinary moments in your life to correct you. He is seeking to bring worth and value out of you. He wants to bring you to personal, relational, and spiritual wholeness. He loves you. God, in His divine Sovereign love, wants to make you authentically holy, like Himself. Every act of discipline, every stripe of correction and disciplinary conversation is designed to bring you to holiness.

Every time Jonah did not learn the lesson God was trying to teach, God was faithful to teach the lesson again.

- Jonah ran from God's call. God pursued Him.

- Jonah fell asleep in the boat. God rocked the boat with a storm and awoke him.

- Jonah fled the Assyrians. God reduced his options until the Assyrians were the only audience Jonah could consider.

- Jonah took pleasure in preaching judgment. God took pleasure in revival.

- Jonah resented God. God gave him a gourd.

- Jonah floundered in bitterness. God called him to holiness.

Often, our bitterness causes us to repeat the same steps in our lives. Our address changes. Our jobs change. Our spouse changes. Our family changes. But the problems remain the same. Mental health experts define insanity as doing the same thing repeatedly with the same results, and doing nothing to change course.

What is the common denominator?

Is it you?

Is the common denominator your own bitter heart?

You see, God is calling us away from bitterness and to holiness. All too often, we resist His call. So, He chastens us. He corrects us. He disciplines us.

God allows you and me, like Jonah, to make the choices of our lives, often driven by a bitter heart, until we trap ourselves in a web of our own design—a web of bitterness. Then He disciplines us with the consequences of our own choices.

We plead for deliverance! He may or may not deliver us, but He will always discipline us. And His discipline has a goal: He wants us to yield to His divine transformation in our lives. God's idea of deliverance and our idea of deliverance may look very different from each other.

Accept His chastening. Embrace the love of correction. Learn the lesson He is teaching, and live like you are His child.

> *"For whom the LORD loves he corrects; even as a father the son in whom he delights."*
> *(Proverbs 3:12 KJV)*

Chapter 5

Bitterness and Prayer: The Laws of Prayer

I remember going to Glacier National Park with my family. The road traversing the park was built by the Civilian Conservation Corps in the 1930's. It's called the *Going to the Sun Highway.* As it climbs the mountains into the interior of the park, the road narrows. It twists and turns. The grand mountain peaks tower in the distance. The steep trail to the narrow heights of Logan Pass stretches out before you. Stunning mountain vistas surround you. The high alpine air is crisp and clear. U-shaped valleys carved by ancient glaciers are covered with a mountain carpet of green. Rocky steeps challenge your imagination as you marvel over God's creation. The mountain goats appear as tiny white dots moving effortlessly above the steep precipice.

These mountains have stood for thousands of years and were long considered impenetrable to human exploration. Courageous workmen carved the narrow, twisting passage out of the stark wilderness. You are now experiencing the harvest of their sacrifice that saw mountains moved.

All too often, we erect mountains of difficulty as we construct and defend the bitterness in our own mental, emotional, and spiritual world. Jonah did. His death grasp on his rights, his expectations, his frustrations, his appraisals and assumptions of other people's motives, and his anger built mountains of bitterness. Jonah's mountains grew larger and larger.

Jonah's mountains of impossibility arose from his prejudice, self-centeredness, arrogance, self-will, and bitterness. His bitter heart positioned Jonah in direct conflict with God. The greatest mountains of our lives are often the ones of our own devising. Like Jonah, our assumptions, presuppositions, and demands create mountains of impossibility. Jesus knows that about us.

Jesus calls us to a journey of faith. There is no quick fix on this journey. Yes, there are crises of faith—at times dramatic—and grace along the way, but the journey of faith will be lifelong. It is not a journey of self-help. It is a journey of faith in God, His ability to deliver, and His passion to transform. God is committed to the long view of grace in your life.

Jesus described our difficulty in Mark 11:22-26 (NKJV).

> *"Have faith in God. For assuredly, I say to you, whoever says to this mountain, 'Be removed and be cast into the sea,' and does not doubt in his heart, but believes that those things he says will be done, he will have whatever he says. Therefore I say to you, whatever things you ask when you pray, believe that you receive them, and you will have them."*

Are you facing some mountains of impossibility in your life? You may have told God how to remove the mountains. You may have pressed your solution upon Him.

His response? "Trust me!"

"Trust you?" we ask. Trust, faith, and obedience are difficult solutions to accept when we are sure we have the right plan of action, if God would only sign off on it!

And He gently presses the issue. "Trust ME."

When God presented His will for Jonah's life, Jonah saw his missionary call to evangelize Nineveh as a mountain range of impossibility. He resisted. He bargained. And then he ran. All the while, God said, "Trust ME."

What about your conversations with God? What about your prayer life? Do you resist His nudges, the gentle pressure that guides you toward His will? Do you beg and bargain with God? All the while, His gentle whisper repeats, "Trust ME."

Ponder this simple God-directed question we must ask about our prayers: "Do you hear me?" If we are to pray prayers that God can hear, what sort of prayers must we pray? Jesus presents us with three laws of prayer, and they will prove to be an outstanding starting point. Jesus' three laws of prayer are faith, fervency, and forgiveness.

Faith

I grew up in a faith-based, home mission work in the foothills of the Appalachian Mountains of Eastern Kentucky. The founders were hardy souls, mostly pioneer women, who carved a frontier ministry of churches and schools out of the rugged landscape of the hill country. Dr. Lela G. McConnell graduated from Asbury College in 1924. Upon her graduation, Dr. H.C. Morrison granted a diploma to the 40-year-old, 5-foot tall evangelist and missionary. Morrison said, "I give this diploma to the

General of the Kentucky Mountains!"

Dr. McConnell fearlessly led this band, largely made up of single ladies, in advancing the cause of Christ and the message of Christian holiness throughout my homeland. She told stories of miracle gas wells and financial provision, how God put food on the table and clothes on the back.

I remember Dr. McConnell well. She gave me my diploma when I graduated from kindergarten, and she called me her baby–a term of endearment reserved for her students. I was nine years old in 1970 when we celebrated her heavenly coronation. In 1979, I graduated from Mount Carmel High School, which Dr. McConnell founded. In 1982, I graduated from the Kentucky Mountain Bible College which she founded in 1931. From 1990 to 2013, I served as a college professor and administrator at KMBC. Dr. McConnell's understanding of radical faith in God seared itself into my consciousness.

During most of my tenure at Kentucky Mountain Bible College, President Phil Speas was my leader. In 2006 we were making plans to build a new chapel. Architectural designs were drawn. Funds were being raised. We had made grant application to a foundation to which I had been introduced during public relations travel for the college. We applied for $200,000. Dr. Speas called the campus family to prayer on a Monday morning. The decision of the grant proposal was pending. We gathered to pray in classroom 201 of the Davis Building. That prayer meeting was mighty. We called on heaven! Our faith was stirred into celebration, although we had not yet seen God's answer.

We left the classroom and returned to the Administration Building to resume our regular Monday morning duties. It was 9:30 when Dr. Speas and I walked through the Administration Building entrance together. We were met by the college librarian who was sorting the mail. She waved an envelope under our noses and said, "I think I have what you are looking for!"

Dr. Speas checked the return address. She was right! The letter was from the foundation to which we had applied. Dr. Speas tore the envelope open to reveal a letter and a check; however, the check was not for the requested $200,000. It was written for $250,000!

We celebrated the miracle of God's supply!

Faith! This kind of faith is a faith in the "efficacy of prayer." This kind of faith means a belief that God is working in response to our prayers.

Jesus positions doubt as the greatest enemy of faith. Doubt means a "divided judgment," a "wavering." And it is rarely a single act; rather, it is an ongoing pattern—an attitude of doubt. Doubt is the opposite of faith. Doubt asks the question, "Does prayer really work?" and fails in its answer.

So Jesus tells us to "Have strong faith" or "Have the strongest faith" (Adam Clarke). This kind of faith is a "continued faith." This kind of faith prevails amid testing. It sees the fulfillment before it happens. Hebrews 11:1 reflects this concept: "Now faith is the substance of things hoped for, the evidence of things not seen."

Mountains represent great difficulties or perplexities in our lives: problems we don't know how to handle. A mountain-moving God is certainly a comfort to a people like us! We are a people who all too often find ourselves grappling with mountains. Dangerous mountains of our own creation loom destructively in our lives. Often we feel like the mountains are beyond our control, and perhaps some are. Mountains of bitterness.

God promises to move mountains!

How?

God promises to move mountains in response to our faith. Sometimes we find ourselves unwilling to bring our problems to God because we know that to which we are clinging is forbidden. We may be clinging to some sin, some right, some expectation, some frustration, or anger. We know that our demands only serve to distance us from the God who loves us, but we insist upon our rights and find ourselves dragged down a path of personal self-destruction.

Then, God's guidance comes. Just as His guidance came to Jonah, His guidance comes to us. The question is, will we accept God's guidance when it comes?

For many years, I have counseled college students, married couples, and others. I enjoyed providing premarital counsel, but marriage counseling was another story! I soon learned that most people who came to me for marriage counseling came when it was already too late. You see, one spouse or the other had already made up their mind as to the course of action they would take, and they simply wanted the counselor to grant them permission to be right!

But to be willing to accept guidance even when we don't like what is being offered means being humble enough, even brave enough, to obey. It takes faith.

Fervency

Jesus' second law of prayer is fervency. Fervency is an enduring quality of believing and receiving. Challenges to faith will rise in front of us. We must possess a fervency of faith that holds on even when obstacles seem to grow in front of our very eyes.

I was on a flight home to Kentucky from Florida a few years ago. I had been to a winter accreditation meeting of the Association for Biblical Higher Education and was accompanied by my Academic Dean. On the way home, we had to land in Cincinnati to get a connecting flight into Lexington. As we neared the runway, I felt the plane dipping its wings back and forth, from left to right. The pilot sought to stabilize the aircraft for landing in a strong crosswind.

Following a successful landing, I exited the plane. I remarked to the pilot, "I prayed for you as you landed this aircraft in the crosswind."

He replied crassly, "Thanks, it worked."

It worked? Is prayer only a pragmatic practice in the midst of crisis? Praying only in crisis treats God like so much superstition... black cats, ladders, broken mirrors, rabbits' feet. Praying only in crisis treats God like Santa Claus Jesus! "My name is Jimmy! I'll take what you gimme!" Surely, Jonah's first prayers uttered from the belly of the great fish must have been selfish, superstitious prayers!

Praying only in crisis imagines God as a marionette on the end of our strings of control. Our rights and expectations become our tools to attempt to control the Creator God of the Universe, turning Him into our own personal servant to dance to our tune. We demand that God protect and approve our self-proclaimed rights and do everything in order to meet our felt needs. Surely, this sort of religion is superstitious paganism. Pagan superstition expressed in Christian jargon. Pagan superstition dressed up with a little make-believe counterfeit Christianity.

Superstition, not worship.

Far too many of us are practicing a version of Christianity that focuses on controlling God rather than worshiping Him. We attempt to manipulate Deity instead of submitting to Him. We may sing the right songs. We may read and quote the right holy book. We may even worship at the right house of worship. But our hearts are far from worship of God. We find ourselves practicing horseshoe religion down at the First Church of the Four Leaf Clover! But superstition is not faith; it is simply our attempt to control our counterfeit deity by demanding our rights.

A fervent faith believes God and receives what He metes out to His worshiper. We must demonstrate a fervency of faith that is willing to receive. This approach to receiving must be one that subscribes to God rather than one that prescribes Him. Do you know the difference between a subscription and a prescription?

I have already introduced you to my brother, James. I am his elder brother by a scant 20 months. When we were boys, around 11 and 12 years old, we became interested in *Sports Illustrated*. At our young ages, we had already become sports fans, most notably of the University of Kentucky Wildcats and the Cincinnati Reds. We found a sub-scription card, pooled our money, and ordered our subscription. We knew nothing about the swimsuit issue; Dad destroyed it before our young minds were scarred by its images.

We subscribed to *Sports Illustrated*. The editors determined its contents.

Subscription.

At least once per year, I fight a bout with allergies. At its worse, it progresses into a sinus infection, bronchitis, and often laryngitis. Laryngitis is an unacceptable option to someone who talks for a living. I am a doctor, but I am not a physician. (I often tell wide-eyed children that I am a doctor of words.) I cannot write a medical prescription for my allergy care. Imagine how foolish if I requested my physician's prescription pad, wrote my own prescription, and demanded the physician's signature!

In the fall of 2013, I was traveling and speaking in Kenya, Africa. My travels took me to the highlands of Kenya where I was in the medical compound community of Ten-wek, just outside the city of Bomet. I was speaking for a minister's conference with over 1000 national pastors in attendance.

One evening after the evening conference session, I dropped by an internet café in the hospital guesthouse where I was staying. A group of physicians was there, visiting and chatting. I heard them complain about patients who visited "Dr. Google," diag-nosed themselves, and then became angry at the live physician for yielding a different diagnosis!

But when most of us seek medical care, we know we must submit to the prescription of the physician. The physician prescribes, and we subscribe to the prescription.

So it should be with prayer. And yet all too often, I have approached God in prayer demanding my rights. My prayers have selfishly focused on having my needs met! I have conjured my own counterfeit idol—myself. I have written the prescription of prayer. Then I arrogantly demand the God of the Universe: "Sign here!"

God will not be cornered with such demanding arrogance mislabeled as prayer!

Fervent faith presents the problem to God, allowing Him to provide the solution in His time and His way. Fervent faith then accepts His solution, His timing, and His Will. Fervent, faith-filled prayer is not so much about changing God as it is about changing me, bringing my will into conformity with His own perfect will. God calls me to submit to His Lordship. Submitting to His Lordship is about subscribing to His prescription. God prescribes. I must simply subscribe in faith.

Our loving Heavenly Father faithfully helps us peel back our tightly gripped fingers, clinging to the vestiges of our rights in our pitiful attempt to control our own lives, our relationships, and even our God. However, our loving God is not forcibly taking. He takes from us that which we freely surrender to Him, and once our hands are open, He fills them to overflowing.

Forgiveness

Jesus' third law of prayer is forgiveness. Forgiveness is a gift from God to be received and extended to others. Jesus calls us to forgive others. Little wonder that *unforgiveness is the secret sin of the church.* Unforgiveness breeds bitterness. Bitterness and anger toward God and others will undermine faith, render prayer ineffective, and result in spiritual separation from God.

A forgiving heart is an essential prerequisite for God to hear and answer our prayers. Jesus said that we must pray,

> *"And forgive us our debts, As we forgive our debtors… For if you forgive men their trespasses, your heavenly Father will also forgive you. But if you do not forgive men their trespasses, neither will your Father forgive your trespasses." (Matthew 6:12, 14-15 NKJV)*

Jesus also said,

> *"Therefore if you bring your gift to the altar, and there remember that your brother has something against you, leave your gift there before the altar, and go your way. First be reconciled to your brother, and then come and offer your gift." (Matthew 5: 23-24 NKJV)*

When I was a boy, I loved riding my bicycle. It gave me freedom to wander, explore, visit friends, show off my skills, and enjoy intoxicating speed. In the 1960s, our family trips to the "Big City" of Lexington, Kentucky, usually included a trip to the Sears & Roebuck store on Vine Street in downtown Lexington. In the early 1970s, Sears moved to the South side of Lexington and took up occupancy in Fayette Mall.

Throughout my childhood, I learned to save money. One day, with the silver dollars, half-dollars, ones, fives, and tens I had collected over a long period of time I determined that I was ready to graduate from a 16-inch bicycle with a banana seat and a sissy bar. That old bike had performed all the wheelies that I was interested in performing. At age 11, I was now interested in speed and adventure. I had saved enough money to buy a new bicycle. Our family ventured to the "Big City." I had one thing on my mind: buying a new bicycle.

Once we arrived at Sears I selected my bike. It was a black 3-speed with handbrakes and 26-inch wheels. I remember plunking my carefully saved money down on the checkout counter. There were silver half-dollars, silver dollars, and paper money. I had saved it all. I spent all fifty dollars and change, and became the proud owner of my grown-up bicycle.

My brother, James, soon graduated to a 26-inch bicycle of his own. We rode together. One day we mounted our bicycles and headed down the "pump-house" hill. We zoomed past the Archer Auditorium and came to a turn in the road. At the turn, the gravel had piled up in windrows. I hit a thick patch of gravel, and my skinny tires skidded. I lost control of the bike and was strewn upon the gravel road. Searing pain cut through my body. My knees turned to shreds as the gravel ripped open my jeans and the flesh beneath. The heels of my palms dug into the gravel as I attempted to spare myself from further injury.

Once I came to a sliding stop, I jumped up in embarrassment. I did not want anyone to witness my incompetence! I quickly assessed the situation. My knee was torn open, bleeding. Rocks and grit ground into flesh. My palms were injured. I dragged my bike out of the gravel road, and hurried inside the mens' bathroom in the Archer Auditorium and gymnasium. I lifted my knee to the sink and rinsed and washed my bloodied knee and hands. I don't remember the ride home, but we made it!

That evening, the wound had stopped bleeding. The clear serum seeped from my body to form a scab on the wound. By morning, my knee was crusty with a tender scab.

Throughout the following days, I was conscious of the wound as it was healing. Momma dressed James and me in Sears Toughskin jeans. A rubber patch was melted to the inside of the knee. The rubber patch annoyed an active boy, because it made his knees sweat! It was even worse with a big, thick, tender scab. I never knew when the Toughskins might grab at my unsuspecting scab, tear it, and start the bleeding all over again.

Our evenings were spent with books, reading aloud, games, and listening to music and entertaining LP records on Dad's stereo console. In those evening hours, seated by the stereo console, I remember pulling up the leg of my Toughskins. The scab itched! The more I rubbed at it, the more it itched. The temptation was consuming! I had to pick at it just a bit! After all, I reasoned, there was some loose stuff, flecks of scab that were ready to fall off, leaving behind the pinkness of newly regenerated skin.

Momma's voice echoes in my ears, "Don't pick at it!"

You know what happened! Suddenly, I went too far. I scratched too deeply. I picked too much. I cut myself to the quick, and the blood started seeping yet again from the stinging wound.

Forgiveness is a lot like my scab-covered knee. The bike wreck had injured me, but I was healing until the Toughskins and my own picking started the bleeding all over again.

Tragedy, devastation, and hurt are to be expected in the sin-cursed world in which we live. Forgiveness is the journey of grace to which Jesus Christ calls us. He calls us to choose to extend the gift of forgiveness to others.

We find ourselves saying, "I don't know why I should forgive them. They won't acknowledge that they did anything wrong! I will simply give them a gift they don't appreciate, and they may even throw it back in my face."

Yet, the persistent call to forgive is repeated by our cruelly mistreated and rejected Lord Jesus Christ.

The cares of life, like my Toughskin jeans, will tear at the wounds of our spirit, tempting us to claim our rights, raise our expectations, vent our frustrations, attribute motives to our offender, embrace anger, and become consumed by bitterness. In the face of the relentless brutality of the temptations of the cares of life, we must continue to choose to forgive.

But there are long, dark nights of the soul, when we are tempted to pull up the leg of our jeans and pick at the scab of hurt and woundedness. We may have even started to heal through extending the gift of forgiveness to our offender, but then we start picking at it! Often, in my hurt, I have found myself picking at the wound that has begun to heal—a wound to which the oil of forgiveness has already been applied. In a moment of weakness and vulnerability, my finger nails of control have moved to massage my wounded rights. It is then that I hear the voice of the Holy Spirit, "Don't pick at it!"

Corrie ten Boom told of not being able to forget a wrong that had been done to her. She had forgiven the person, but she kept rehashing the incident and so couldn't sleep. Finally, Corrie cried out to God for help. "His help came in the form of a kindly Lutheran pastor," Corrie wrote, "to whom I confessed my failure after two sleepless weeks."

"Up in the church tower," he said, nodding out the window, "is a bell which is rung by pulling on a rope. But you know what? After the sexton lets go of the rope, the bell keeps on swinging. First ding, then dong. Slower and slower until there's a final dong and it stops. I believe the same thing is true of forgiveness. When we forgive, we take our hand off the rope. But if we've been tugging at our grievances for a long time, we mustn't be surprised if the old angry thoughts keep coming for a while. They're just the ding-dongs of the old bell slowing down."

"And so it proved to be. There were a few more midnight reverberations, a couple of dings when the subject came up in my conversations, but the force—which was my willingness in the matter—had gone out of them. They came less and less often and at the last stopped altogether..."

Forgiveness is a choice. Once made, it must be lived out as a continued act of the will.

We must forgive to be forgiven. Jesus teaches us that the gift of forgiveness is one that can be received only as it is given away. Giving away the gift of forgiveness is a volitional releasing of my rights to the Lordship of Jesus Christ. Jesus demands that we forgive others for our own soul's sake. The professing Christian who resists giving the gift of forgiveness will soon destroy his or her own profession of faith through clinging to the rights of resentment and bitterness. The joy of the Lord will dissipate into a destructive spiritual loss.

I have often heard people say, "I've forgiven others, but I just can't forgive myself." Early in my ministry with Bible College young people, I remember encouraging a few who were haunted by guilt and shame that they simply needed to forgive themselves. I had heard the message of self-forgiveness taught by media pop psychologists. It seemed natural just to layer it on top of my Christian understanding of forgiveness. These young people had already trusted Christ's forgiveness, and now they needed to forgive themselves, or so I taught.

Soon, I realized the weakness of this position. I have made it my practice to read through the Bible nearly every year for a number of years now. As I reflected upon the whole of Scripture, I queried, "Where in Scripture is the concept of self-forgiveness taught?" My reflections did not identify a single instance of Scripture teaching the notion of self-forgiveness. I have heard Oprah teach it. I have heard Dr. Phil teach it. But not Scripture.

Over years of pondering and reflection, I have come to realize that the notion of self-forgiveness is filled with self-pity, weakness, and an absence of faith. You don't need to forgive yourself!

Think of it this way. Could you die on a cross and shed your blood to effectuate forgiveness for anyone? Of course not! Could any degree of your personal suffering, degradation, self-mortification, self-flagellation or spiritual works ever achieve your own salvation or that of another? Of course not! Neither can you suffer enough or wallow in enough self-pity and regret to muster any sort of self-forgiveness.

I met Gail during my evangelistic travels. She remembered me from my childhood. Gail had been a boarding student at Mount Carmel High School when I was a toddler. She loved and admired my parents, their marriage, and my dad's teaching of mathematics.

Each service, Gail sat near the front of the church. Her face was incredibly expressive. When I told a funny story, I was guaranteed a response from Gail. When God directed me to share a particularly penetrating thought that struck home with Gail, she would wince with the awareness of that truth.

After nightly services, a group of friends joined together for dinner. We went to various restaurants in town, told stories, laughed, and enjoyed Christian fellowship. Gail was always ready to lead the way with a hearty laugh and a ready smile. Gail was enjoying life in Christ.

But Gail had some deep pain.

I could see the pain in her eyes. In church services, I saw the flash of pain and regret. At dinner and in conversation, there it was again. Gradually, Gail's story tumbled out.

Gail had grown up at Trinity Friends Church. She had met Dr. Lela McConnell there, and was drawn by her charisma to attend Mount Carmel Christian High School. At Mount Carmel, Gail flourished. She grew in her Christian walk, and even sensed a call to children's ministry. Gail met and married a man with whom she attended high school. He was not who she thought him to be. Gail's call to ministry was soon foiled by a bad marriage to a man whom she learned was far from God.

Gail and her husband moved to the West Coast. Soon, she herself was far from God. Gail experimented with other religions, and settled upon New Age philosophy. She raised her children without any Christian values.

In her 60's, Gail's marriage had ended in divorce. She longed for home. Gail moved east. Gail's journey east was also a journey back to the God she had known as a teen. Now single, her children raised, Gail returned to the church of her childhood. That was when we met.

It was obvious to me that Gail was walking with Jesus. Her journey had brought her back to God. Gail was working as a volunteer in children's ministry in the Church. Her gifts were apparent. It was also obvious that Gail was deeply pained.

During the revival meeting, I preached a message in which I developed the idea of the futility of self-forgiveness. Gail's eyes reflected shock when I said, "You don't have to forgive yourself." I went on to explain that Jesus is the only sinless Lamb of God who can provide forgiveness. As we look to the sacrificial death and atonement of Jesus Christ on the Cross of Calvary we gain some understanding of the awfulness of sin. We gain an appreciation of the atonement which Jesus provides and our own utter helplessness. In the light of the Cross, it becomes clear that none of us can do anything to provide forgiveness for ourselves. Only through faith in the Lamb of God and the merits of His atoning grace can forgiveness be received by faith.

I suppose that some people use the expression "You just have to forgive yourself" to connote a surrender to God or a personal letting-go; but the language of self-help is grossly inadequate to express the awfulness of sin, our desperate need of a Savior, and the necessity of our placing faith in Jesus Christ, not in any actions conceived or contrived in oneself.

At the close of the service, Gail came forward, bowed at the altar, and prayed a prayer of brokenness. When she rose from prayer, she was bright. A burden had been lifted.

Gail told me of her wanderings, pain, and brokenness. She then told me of the journey of forgiveness. She was clearly aware of Jesus' forgiveness of her and of her forgiveness of others, but she lived with regret. Gail's regret was for a life poorly lived. Her regret was for what might have been, and Gail felt that she had to forgive herself for her failures.

You see, secular culture had preached the message of self-forgiveness to Gail. She had been told, "Just forgive yourself." But she couldn't. Her shame and regret were too great. She later reflected, "What a weight was lifted that night! I just praise The Lord that He sent you to Trinity Friends Church!"

The Word of God to Gail was, "You don't have to forgive yourself. You cannot! You must simply look to Jesus in faith for what He has already done on the cross, and trust His forgiving power!"

That night at revival meeting in Gail's home church, her shame and regret were nailed to the cross of Jesus Christ. The sins of her past that she could never forgive were already forgiven in Jesus Christ! Gail must simply look to Him in faith!

Many of us have confessed, repented, and accepted Christ's forgiveness. But regret, consequences of past sins, and strained relationships caused by our sins against others provide cruel reminders of the brokenness of sin. We try to muster grace to live in forgiveness, but we don't feel any better! Someone says, "Forgive yourself," but that only leads to emptiness. What must we do? We must look to Jesus to move the mountains in our lives. The sacrifice of the sinless Son of God upon the cross of Calvary is enough! His shed blood is the atoning sacrifice for our sins, our brokenness, and our regret. He provides wholeness, healing, and peace. We must simply look to Him, not ourselves, in faith for His forgiveness.

God longs to move our mountains, but we have a role in that. All too often, we face the obstruction of a mountain of our own creation. We erect that mountain of opposition by clinging to our own rights, holding unrealistic expectations of others, allowing corresponding frustrations to creep into our thoughts, making appraisals as to others' ignoble motives, living in anger, and spiraling downward into ever encroaching bitterness.

"Have faith in God. For assuredly, I say to you, whoever says to this mountain, 'Be removed and be cast into the sea,' and does not doubt in his heart, but believes that those things he says will be done, he will have whatever he says. Therefore I say to you, whatever things you ask when you pray, believe that you receive them, and you will have them. And whenever you stand praying, if you have anything against anyone, forgive him, that your Father in heaven may also forgive you your trespasses. But if you do not forgive, neither will your Father in heaven forgive your trespasses." (Mark 11:22-26 NKJV)

Are you struggling with a lack of faith? Perhaps you need to pray, "Lord I believe, help thou my unbelief!" We must trust Him explicitly in unwavering faith.

Are you failing to hold on in fervency? Do you find yourself substituting your own answer instead of waiting for God's answer? Are you prescribing God instead of subscribing to him? We must hold on to Him fervently, believing in Him to move the mountain in His time and His way.

Have you become prayerless? Have you allowed other things to crowd out communion with God? We must be aggressively obedient to walk in God's clearly revealed light in our lives or that light becomes darkness. Prayerless living will render us spiritually powerless and will make us weak and susceptible to temptation.

Is your heart battling bitterness? You know you should forgive. You may have even tried to in the past. Has a bitter spirit crept back in, supplanting the Spirit of God? We must extend forgiveness to others if we are to receive God's forgiveness. Only the heart that is aligned with God in the spirit of forgiveness can exercise a fervency of faith to believe God to move mountains.

The biblical record of Jonah's life and ministry leaves us hanging. The story is unresolved. We don't see Jonah arriving at a place where his heart is aligned in submission with the heart of God. At the close of Jonah 4, his prayers appear to remain largely ineffectual. But is that the end of Jonah's story? Does the story of his personal failure to forgive hint at something more?

God is working within you to heal your hurts, cleanse your bitterness, and make you spiritually whole. Spiritually whole people communicate wholeness in their relationships with others, and they can pray—really pray.

Faith, fervency, and forgiveness will lead you on a path so that you can pray prayers that God can hear. Such praying will empower you to keep your rights surrendered to Jesus Christ and prevent you from the downward spiral into bitterness. These are prayers that God hears.

Chapter 6

The Biblical Solution to the Problem of Bitterness

Jonah was a bitter prophet. Jonah's bitterness poisoned his own soul, spoiled his relationships with others, and created a barrier between himself and his loving Heavenly Father.

People at varying stages of Christian life and experience respond differently to the issues of rights, expectations, corresponding frustrations, assumptions of others' motives, and anger which leads to bitterness.

Paul describes three different types of people in I Corinthians.

> *"For what man knows the things of a man except the spirit of the man which is in him? Even so no one knows the things of God except the Spirit of God. Now we have received, not the spirit of the world, but the Spirit who is from God, that we might know the things that have been freely given to us by God.*

> *"These things we also speak, not in words which man's wisdom teaches but which the Holy Spirit teaches, comparing spiritual things with spiritual. But the **natural** man does not receive the things of the Spirit of God, for they are foolishness to him; nor can he know them, because they are spiritually discerned. But he who is spiritual judges all things, yet he himself is rightly judged by no one. For 'who has known the mind of the Lord that he may instruct Him?' But we have the mind of Christ.*

> *"And I, brethren, could not speak to you as to **spiritual** people but as to **carnal**, as to babes in Christ. I fed you with milk and not with solid food; for until now you were not able to receive it, and even now you are still not able; for you are still carnal. For where there are envy, strife, and divisions among you, are you not carnal and behaving like mere men?" (emphasis mine)*

(I Corinthians 2:11-3:3 KJV)

Paul describes the natural person, the carnal person, and the spiritual person. The natural person is lost and without Jesus. The natural person is without faith, and as a result, is more susceptible to bitterness.

The carnal person is double-minded. The carnal person has experienced the new birth but is labeled as carnal, fleshly, and unspiritual. The carnal person has repented of sin and found forgiveness and salvation by faith; however, this born-again person still struggles with the carnal mind. This remnant of unbelief allies itself with bitterness. The carnal tendencies bend the soul with a selfish, unspiritual warp that curves the carnal believer back on himself or herself. The unspiritual magnetism of a fallen moral nature, a remnant of the "old man" in the heart of a new believer, wrestles with a double-mind of devotion.

The mature, spiritually-minded believer is able to appropriate grace to resist and rise above even intense temptation. The spiritual person is still susceptible to mighty temptations toward bitterness; however, the abiding fullness of the Holy Spirit will sensitize the faithful to resist temptation, to repent when necessary, and to adjust one's attitude when one indulges temptations of bitterness.

The believer's cure for bitterness begins with surrender to the Lordship of Christ. The born-again child of God is called into a relationship of intimacy with Christ that will demand the complete surrender of our rights to Him. This complete surrender includes the surrender of my right to expect others to understand me or meet my needs. It reaches to my professional life, and includes a surrender of the right to expect others to do tasks my way.

Once we have exclusively surrendered to the Lordship of Jesus Christ, faith must be exercised toward God to redirect our expectations. Faith directs our expectations away from people and toward God. People will disappoint us. We must have faith in God.

William Carey said: "Expect great things from God. Attempt great things for God."

Expectations.

Assumptions of others' motives stem from expectations. Scripture calls us to resist the temptation to judge another person's motive. The Bible teaches "For the LORD does not see as man sees; for man looks at the outward appearance, but the LORD looks at the heart" (I Samuel 16:7 NKJV).

The victorious Christian, living in the fullness of the Holy Spirit, will find the empowerment of the perfect love which John describes in his first epistle (I John 3:1, 4:7-21). Perfect love empowers right relationships, right attitudes, right thinking, and necessary adjustments. This sort of holiness is not automatic; it is based in intimacy and fellowship with a Triune God. This sort of holiness is lived out humbly with a constant awareness of the need for obedience.

As a child, I often heard my mother say, "Life is a series of attitudes and adjustments." And it is. The call to holy living is a call to live surrendered to the Lordship of Jesus Christ. It is a call to the self-abandoned life where one's rights are submitted to His Lordship. It is a call to a life of faith where one's expectations are based in Christ's Lordship. This call to holy living draws us beyond the relational frustrations of assumptions and judgment directed toward others. Our holy calling beckons us past anger and bitterness. Our holy calling is to a life of perfect love lived out through the impetus of the fullness of the indwelling Holy Spirit.

> "I beseech you therefore, brethren, by the mercies of God, that you present your bodies a living sacrifice, holy, acceptable to God, which is your reasonable service. And do not be conformed to this world, but be transformed by the renewing of your mind, that you may prove what is that good and acceptable and perfect will of God." (Romans 12:1-2 KJV)

Someone has said that "the trouble with living sacrifices is that they tend to crawl off the altar!" The practicality of the simple truth of perfect love is that Christ calls us to a life of surrender, sacrifice, and service. He calls us to surrender ourselves to Himself and obey.

I can testify to the joy of the surrendered life. I can witness to the transformation of the Spirit in my life. I can verify the validity of hope in a life lived beyond the brokenness of bitterness. I pray that you might know this joy! Surrender your rights and expectations, and get on the path to Christ's work of perfect love in your heart!

Chapter 7

Is Holiness Optional?

So there's Brother Jonah under the gourd. He has traced the entire course of the cycle of bitterness. Clinging to his rights fed his expectations, engendering frustration, unholy appraisals of others, anger, and full-blown bitterness. Bitterness and depression haunt the prophet.

So what about you and me? Here we are. We have come face to face with the issues of bitterness. We have confronted Biblical teaching that challenges and arrests us. What will you do with this truth? You may find yourself saying, "These teachings sound too good to be true."

"Nobody can live that way!"

"The Bible does not require that kind of holiness from people!"

"After all, we all sin every day!"

If these objections are yours and you have stayed with this book long enough to get to this chapter, then I want to invite you on a further journey of ideas. This journey is one of questions that the Hebrew author entertains. We will make these questions and ideas our own.

Here are some big questions. What are my options? Do I really have to live this surrendered life? Does God really expect me to live a life with my rights abandoned to His Lordship? Does God really expect me to live a life with my expectations and faith based in Him, and not in other people? Can God do something in my heart and life so that I can rest in that kind of reality and no longer suffer from chronic bitterness?

If I don't pursue this kind of surrendered life where my rights and expectations are yielded to Christ, what are my options? If I pursue a life of frustration, anger, and bitterness, what are my options then? Everyone else seems to live that life of selfishness, why can't I? What are my options?

Fair enough. These are all good questions.

It was the last week of April. Friday night of that week, Hazel and Monty, our first two miniature dachshunds, joined our family. But the week is memorable because of four Bible college students–two couples whom I was teaching and mentoring.

First one couple and then a second came to my office. Both confessed episodes of immorality, sin, and brokenness to me. Shudders of sorrow and grief wracked my body as I heard their stories of sin and immorality. How could this happen? Even today, I grieve the brokenness that sin brought to those precious young lives.

During that season of grief, I fled to God's Word. As I read Hebrews 12, I suddenly saw some answers—some explanation. Doubtful at first, I began to explore the simple truth that seemed too great to understand. I read it again and again. I began to make connections, to test the Word, and to teach it to others.

The passage that spoke so profoundly to me was Hebrews 12:14-17:

> *"Pursue peace with all people, and holiness, without which no one will see the Lord: looking carefully lest anyone fall short of the grace of God; lest any root of bitterness springing up cause trouble, and by this many become defiled; lest there be any fornicator or profane person like Esau, who for one morsel of food sold his birthright. For you know that afterward, when he wanted to inherit the blessing, he was rejected, for he found no place for repentance, though he sought it diligently with tears."* (NKJV)

The question with which Scripture confronts us is this: "Is holiness optional?" If I don't pursue holiness, what are my options? The Hebrew writer lays out our options very clearly in this passage. If the believer fails to pursue holiness, he or she will be destroyed by the pressures and pulls of life. The only options are holiness or bitterness, holiness or defilement, holiness or sensuality/sexual immorality, and holiness or rejection by God.

The command of God's Word is that we follow after holiness. We are exhorted to run swiftly to reach the goals of peace and purity. But there are pitfalls along the way. There are deliberate and deceptive steps that take us away from the pursuit of holiness. We must pursue holiness.

On an individual level, it is either holiness or bitterness.

The Hebrew writer is warning us against idolaters who enter a community of faith, pursue strange gods, encourage others to do so, and become a poisonous influence on the community. The warning is against the corrupting influence of the "root of bitterness" of idolatry.

Richard Taylor explains (*Beacon Bible Commentary*) that the bitterness is more than unpleasant. It is poisonous. He indicates that the root of bitterness in a church is the person who falls short of holiness, thereby threatening the health of the church. Taylor takes a step further and identifies this root of bitterness as the carnal mind, the inherited sin disposition, the moral warp in human nature, the unspiritual magnetism, the old man, the body of sin, inherited depravity.

The Hebrew writer seems to suggest that no one can be a root of bitterness in his church relationships unless that one has a root of bitterness in his own heart. If each of us is born with this inherited unspiritual magnetism, then each of us who fails to pursue a Biblical solution to the problem of bitterness is threatened by spiritual destruction. Our neglect to press on to holiness may create a threat even to the well-being of the church.

Taylor emphasizes that our neglect to pursue a heart cleansed from the "root of bitterness" exposes us to a danger of an eruption of the venom of self-will that will defile others.

What is this cycle of bitterness that the Hebrew writer describes? Many of us have faced hurts that have scarred and wounded us. We know that if we dwell on the hurts, the pain will fester and grow fruit of bitterness in our lives. Hurt creates wounds. Untreated and unhealed wounds of the spirit will grow into anger, resentment, and eventually bitterness. Bitterness is deceptive. Satan deceives us to think that our bitterness will hurt the person against whom we are bitter; however, the person enduring the greatest hurt is the one who harbors bitterness.

Dr. Nelson Perdue says, "Those who live in the deception of sin will die in the darkness of the soul."

Bitterness and holiness cannot coexist.

In 2013, I was in Kenya, Africa, speaking to pastors. I told the story this way. Suppose that a stray kitten was dropped off near your home. You felt compassion for the kitten and adopted it. It was in a terrible, flea-bitten state when you took it in. You fed Kitty. You took Kitty to the vet, got it its shots, and nursed it to health. You talked to Kitty, petted Kitty, and nurtured it. Almost imperceptibly, Kitty grows to adulthood. One day you come home from work and Kitty bares its claws and extends its fangs. Kitty turns on you and eats you alive! What you didn't know was what you thought was just a simple house cat was really a wild lion! And now it's all grown up.

That's bitterness. It feels so good when it's small. We pet it, stroke it, and nurture it, but before we know it, it grows to its adult size. Bitterness will be true to its nature and will certainly consume us alive! All too soon, bitterness destroys you.

Nelson Perdue says, "Sin never stays the same size. It grows on what it feeds on... The nature of sin is such that it destroys your capacity to know its progress." The kitty cat of bitterness becomes a lion of destruction, and you didn't know when it grew up!

On one occasion, I made a Facebook post regarding the topic of bitterness. My friend, Brooke Thelander responded, "Bitterness is a poison that we drink expecting someone else to get sick."

I have spent a number of years in itinerant ministry. At times it seems I am in a different church every Sunday. I hear the stories. I see bitterness and its consequences played out before me. Did you know that bitterness is the secret sin of the church? A lack of clear teaching on the Biblical solution to bitterness has nurtured a spirit of bitterness across the church world that all too often tears us apart. Tragically, bitterness has become the "new normal" in many of our church, family, and professional relationships.

Bitterness requires no choice whatsoever. The difficult choice is not to become bitter. Bitterness is the default option of the fallen human condition. Our inherited sinful disposition with which we were born is an unspiritual magnetism that attracts us toward bitterness. Bitterness will happen in each human's life unless choices of grace are made to prevent it.

The first step toward the solution for bitterness is a genuine experience of the new birth. This sort of spiritual conversion demands a sense of conviction of conscience that bitterness is sin. Bitterness demands forgiveness. I cannot continue to enjoy a witness of the Spirit that I am growing in the grace of God as one of His born again children if I persist in harboring an unforgiving spirit. Jesus said, "For if you forgive men their trespasses, your heavenly Father will also forgive you. But if you do not forgive men their trespasses, neither will your Father forgive your trespasses." (Matthew 6:14-15 NKJV).

In response to Christ's forgiveness, He demands that I extend forgiveness to others. Forgiveness is a gift from God that I can only keep as I give it away! I must follow Christ's call to forgive others.

In 1999, my friend, Evangelist Lane Loman, preached a message on forgiveness at Sebring Camp, Sebring, Ohio. In it he gave four proofs of forgiveness. You know you have forgiven someone when: 1) your ill feelings toward them are gone, and you see them through Jesus' eyes, 2) you care about them and what they are doing to themselves more than what they did to you and your feelings, 3) you rejoice in their successes, and 4) you stop talking about them.

But forgiveness is not enough!

The Hebrew writer is teaching the Hebrew Christians that even after conversion, they struggle with a personal "root of bitterness" which must be cleansed from the heart. Inherited sin is this "root of bitterness." This moral warp has so infected the human race, resulting in a duplicitous moral nature, that each of us is called to a personal cleansing from this "root of bitterness."

Only as this nature is confessed and crucified upon the cross of Christ may the believer be freed from its all-infecting influence.

Paul wrote,

> "But if, while we seek to be justified by Christ, we ourselves also are found sinners, is Christ therefore a minister of sin? Certainly not! For if I build again those things which I destroyed, I make myself a transgressor. For I through the law died to the law that I might live to God. **I have been crucified with Christ;** it is no longer I who live, but Christ lives in me; and the life which I now live in the flesh I live by faith in the Son of God, who loved me and gave Himself for me. I do not set aside the grace of God; for if righteousness comes through the law, then Christ died in vain." (Galatians 2:17-21 NKJV, [emphasis mine])

The question before us is this, *Is holiness optional?*

Once one takes the first step down the path of bitterness, the second step is obvious. *On a corporate level, it's either holiness or defilement.*

One cannot stay bitter alone very long. We find ourselves validating our bitterness to others. Our tongues wag. We seek others to align with our bitterness. We want others to be complicit in confirming our point of view and shoring up our own identity. After all, I must be right!

Personal bitterness becomes corporate defilement. One person takes up another's offense. The cancer spreads. The church splits. The campus splinters. Spreading bitterness in corporate defilement is an act of disobedience to the call to peace and holiness. Corporate peace is the fruit of personal holiness. Corporate defilement, hostility, and division is anti-holy.

Churches never split over the color of the carpet; churches split over a root of bitterness and carnal control! A bitter heart filled with carnality can spread enough poison to defile an entire church. Factions develop. A carnal conflict escalates. Each is susceptible to the temptation toward bitterness, no matter how well filled with the Holy Spirit. But a carnal, unsanctified heart possesses an unspiritual magnetism that is spiritually attracted toward the path of bitterness, because there's a root of bitterness within the heart.

I have seen bitterness in homes where children have grown up with "roast preacher" served every Sunday for Sunday dinner. It is no wonder that church-attending children from homes laced with bitterness want nothing to do with the church when they reach adulthood.

I have seen bitterness in parsonage homes where pastors' children have been exposed to too much pain and hurt. Perhaps the pastor father failed to protect his children from the hurt. Perhaps he openly criticized church members. However it happened, bitterness took root. One friend from my youth nurtured such bitterness. His bitterness found its origin in a desire to protect his parents from hurt. In adulthood, this son of a preacher became a full blown alcoholic and blamed his alcoholism upon a church hierarchy that mistreated his pastor parents.

Scripture offers a cure for the corporate defilement created by bitterness. The solution begins with addressing one's own spiritual need. Humbly seeking God's forgiveness and the forgiveness of those wronged marks a path of genuine restoration. Humbled by Christ's gift of forgiveness, we must give the gift of forgiveness away to those who have wronged us. Forgiveness is a gift that must be given away if the giver is to continue to possess it.

Christ longs to replace personal bitterness and corporate defilement with a spirit of perfect love.

> *"And above all things have fervent love for one another, for love will cover a multitude of sins." (I Peter 4:8 NKJV).*

The Apostle of Love reminds us, "Behold what manner of love the Father has bestowed on us, that we should be called children of God! Therefore the world does not know us, because it did not know Him" (I John 3:1 KJV). John continues: "Herein is our love made perfect, that we may have boldness in the day of judgment: because as he is, so are we in this world. There is no fear in love; but perfect love casteth out fear: because fear hath torment. He that feareth is not made perfect in love." (I John 4:17-18 KJV).

When bitterness defiles the Body of Christ, its infection spreads rapidly. I remember some Christian college students who were called into the ministry. Both young men testified to a call to preach. Roommates, they began spewing their frustration and anger to each other. The spirit of criticism multiplied into anger. Before the evening was over these fellows became so critical and angry that they left campus, traveled to an adjoining county and bought a 12-pack of beer. As they drank, the old spirit of their lives before Christ began to wash over their souls.

Bitterness spreads to defile others. Once I choose to walk away from God's standard of holiness, I find myself embracing bitterness.

Corporate defilement next advances its infection to the relational level. *On a relational level, it is either holiness or sensuality, and often sexual immorality.*

When I was plunged into a context of ministry in which I witnessed the broken lives of young people caught in the clutches of sexual immorality, I initially questioned the apparent spiritual connection between bitterness, defilement, and sexual immorality. So I tested the theory of what I thought the Bible was teaching. Over the years, when I have talked with people who are caught in the brokenness of sexual immorality, I asked them this question: "Is there anybody in your life against whom you are bitter?"

As I tested the connection of scripture and what I thought I was seeing in the passage, my understanding of the teaching of scripture has been validated. One hundred percent of those interviewed indicated that personal bitterness against someone or something preceded their immoral conduct.

We live in a 21st-century cultural and religious context that is broken by sensuality and sexual immorality. For some, accumulating possessions dominates life pursuits. For others, the pursuit of sexual immorality is the sensuality of choice. We need the holiness of God to reign in our hearts and keep us clean from bitterness, defilement, and sensuality.

Tragically, we experience proliferating sexual brokenness in both the pulpit and the pew because we are not proclaiming a Biblical call to live differently. We reject life in the Spirit and embrace a sensual, idolatrous version of Christianity. As sexual impropriety abounds in the pulpit, sexual brokenness proliferates in the church.

Our situation is not all that different from the situation Paul confronted in the first-century church.

Paul wrote the Thessalonian church:

> *"For this is the will of God, your sanctification: that you should abstain from sexual immorality; that each of you should know how to possess his own vessel in sanctification and honor, not in passion of lust, like the Gentiles who do not know God; that no one should take advantage of and defraud his brother in this matter, because the Lord is the avenger of all such, as we also forewarned you and testified. For God did not call us to uncleanness, but in holiness. Therefore he who rejects this does not reject man, but God, who has also given us His Holy Spirit."*

> *(I Thessalonians 4:3-8 NKJV)*

Paul exhorted the Ephesian church similarly:

> *"Therefore be imitators of God as dear children. And walk in love, as Christ also has loved us and given Himself for us, an offering and a sacrifice to God for a sweet-smelling aroma. But fornication and all uncleanness or covetousness, let it not even be named*

among you, as is fitting for saints; neither filthiness, nor foolish talking, nor coarse jesting, which are not fitting, but rather giving of thanks. For this you know, that no fornicator, unclean person, nor covetous man, who is an idolater, has any inheritance in the kingdom of Christ and God. Let no one deceive you with empty words, for because of these things the wrath of God comes upon the sons of disobedience. Therefore do not be partakers with them. (Ephesians 5:1-7 NKJV)

Esau provides the Hebrew author with a picture of a life dominated by sensuality. The narrative reaches back to the first book of the Bible, describing Esau as impulsive, dominated by appetite.

"Now Jacob cooked a stew; and Esau came in from the field, and he was weary. And Esau said to Jacob, 'Please feed me with that same red stew, for I am weary.' Therefore his name was called Edom.

But Jacob said, 'Sell me your birthright as of this day.'

And Esau said, 'Look, I am about to die; so what is this birthright to me?'

Then Jacob said, 'Swear to me as of this day.'

So he swore to him, and sold his birthright to Jacob. And Jacob gave Esau bread and stew of lentils; then he ate and drank, arose, and went his way. Thus Esau despised his birthright."

(Genesis 25:29-34 NKJV)

Esau was not disciplined by an ability to delay his gratification. He made a bad bargain. He had to have his red bean soup. And forever after, the red, hairy one named Esau, bore a nickname—Edom—as a term of derision and constant reminder of his weak character. Esau's immorality was displayed when he took Canaanite wives, breaking his parents' hearts.

Nelson Perdue says, "While we may become intellectual giants, we are moral pygmies... If you change your standard of morality, the first thing you must change is your concept of God." Such was the sin of Esau.

God is a holy God, and He requires "holiness, without which no man shall see the Lord." He demands a different path from the routine of the broader culture. If we are to be cured of our immorality, we must be a people of holiness. The cure for immorality is implied by the Hebrew author in our passage. A radical repentance that includes God's forgiveness and restoration from an immoral life must lead to a full surrender and cleansing from the inherited depravity.

Is holiness optional? Holiness must impact our lives on an individual level, cleansing us from the root of bitterness; on a corporate level, cleansing from defilement; on a relational level, cleansing us from sensuality and sexual immorality; and finally, if we fail to seek holiness, it will impact us vertically in our relationship with God. Rejecting the grace of holiness results in being rejected by God.

A case study in Esau is warranted. Esau was the twin son of Isaac and Rebecca. His brother Jacob stayed about the family tents. Jacob was his momma's boy. Esau was a man of the woods and the field, hunting and exploring.

Jacob was cooking the pot of red bean soup, when Esau came home, famished from the hunt. Esau demanded that Jacob serve him.

Jacob, ever the trickster and conniver demanded, "What's in it for me?"

Jacob kept pushing. He knew his brother's weakness.

"I want your birthright," Jacob demanded. The birthright was the larger portion of the inheritance that the firstborn son would receive.

"What is my birthright worth to me if I die from hunger?" Esau insisted. Gratification must be instant for Esau.

Jacob seized the moment, bartered a trade, and Esau is forever marked as a fool.

Esau's domination (Genesis 25:32) was carnality. He embraced an "end justifies the means" worldview that demanded satisfaction of his immediate desires. His need for instant gratification increased Esau's appetite for the sensual. He married foreign wives (Genesis 26:34). This act of haste broke his parents' hearts, as Esau circumvented their provision of a wise and appropriate marriage partner.

Further, Esau would become known as an entirely sensual man, who sold his birthright to relieve his temporary appetite. He lived a life in opposition to holiness, a future sold cheaply for self-gratification. He neglected holiness, sought pleasure in immorality, and sacrificed the holiness of God on the altar of self-gratification.

Esau's desire was self-interest. He would say that he desired his inheritance rights—holiness, the inheritance rights of us all; but, tragically, Esau wanted to use God to satisfy his own desires.

Esau's destiny was rejection by God. Nelson Perdue says, "The same truth that shows us the way out and gives us life, if ignored, will destroy us." If our deepest values are ignored often enough, there is a point of no return. The thing that assuages our appetite is forgotten but the consequences of our foolhardiness remains.

The question before us is direct and pointed. *"Is holiness optional?"* The only options are bitterness, corporate defilement, sensuality and sexual immorality, and ultimate rejection by God. None of these is a valid option. Each is destruction, and bitterness is the first step.

What are the areas of sensuality that tempt you? "For all that is in the world—the lust of the flesh, the lust of the eyes, and the pride of life—is not of the Father but is of the world" (I John 2:16 NKJV). The lust of the flesh, which is sexual immorality, is a dominant temptation of youth. Such temptation never entirely dissipates with maturity and aging. The lust of the eyes, the covetous accumulation of material possessions, is a potent and tempting appeal of mid-life. Pride of life appeals to lust for power, position, and control, and serves as a dominant temptation of those in senior years.

The only options are holiness or bitterness, holiness or defilement, holiness or sexual immorality, and holiness or rejection by God. Those sound like no options at all to me. "Follow peace with all men and holiness, without which no man shall see the Lord." Nelson Perdue says, "Holiness is more than a doctrine to be taught, it is a life to be lived."

Bruce Larson worked in New York City in the RCA Building on Fifth Avenue. He liked to bring guests to see a gigantic statue of Atlas located at the entrance. Atlas is featured as a beautifully proportioned man who, with all his muscles bulging and straining, is holding the world upon his shoulders. The most powerful man in the world can barely carry the burden of the world upon his shoulders. Larson then directs his guests' attention to the other side of Fifth Avenue where in Saint Patrick's Cathedral, behind the high altar, is a little statue of the boy Jesus, perhaps eight or nine years old, who with no effort holds the world in one hand.

That thorny issue of clinging to one's rights has suddenly resurfaced. The same issue that drove Jonah's cycle of bitterness, rears its ugly head in our lives too!

Do you see the choice that confronts us? We can carry our burden of bitterness and let it drag us down a personal path of destruction. Or we can abandon ourselves, beginning with our personal rights, to the Lordship of Jesus Christ. We are confronted with a choice which demands our surrender.

We have options! But they are not acceptable ones, are they?

What is your decision? Will you abandon your rights to Jesus? Will you surrender the world that you are grappling, off-balance, to control?

Holiness is the *only* way to live!

"Now may the God of peace Himself sanctify you completely; and may your whole

spirit, soul, and body be preserved blameless at the coming of our Lord Jesus Christ. He who calls you is faithful, who also will do it." (I Thess. 5:23-24 NKJV).

Chapter 8

Are You Uncomfortable Yet?

Here is an interesting question: "Who wrote the Book of Jonah?"

Scholars disagree. Contemporary scholars suggest various theories. I suppose that I am traditional and simple enough to accept the historicity of Jonah as the author of the book that bears his name.

For arguments' sake, humor me. What does Jonah's authorship of his own testimony suggest? How about some informed speculation? I think that Jonah's authorship suggests that the prophet lived on past the recorded events of the book. It seems to me that his authorship suggests that Jonah repented of his racist, prejudiced disobedience. In fact, his authorship suggests that Jonah allowed God to change his heart, and that he enjoyed a spiritual recovery from bitterness. Otherwise, why would he tell us such a story as the one recorded?

There is hope in Jonah's story. There can be hope in your story as well. Your story can be one of hope and spiritual recovery from bitterness.

Allow me to suggest some simple lessons from Jonah. First, the Bible tells some stories that are very uncomfortable to tell. We are uncomfortable with Jonah's racism and bigotry, along with his disobedience to God, because Jonah may show us ourselves. We are uncomfortable with God's judgment on Jonah, because it may show us God's judgment on our own attitudes and actions. We are uncomfortable with Jonah's clinging to his rights, expectations, frustration, judgment of others, and anger, because Jonah may prophesy how wrong we are when we proceed through the same broken cycle.

Second, uncomfortable stories need to be told. How can we teach and learn from one another unless we embrace the transparency of telling our stories? Such is the beauty of Christian discipleship. We do not have to learn every broken and destructive lesson from direct experience, if we will accept the discipleship that other believers' stories offer us.

Third, each of us has uncomfortable stories to tell. Clinging to our rights is part of the narrative of the human journey. Each of us has behaved selfishly and foolishly. Many of life's greatest lessons from God are often learned in the midst of our most uncomfortable stories. Our stubborn refusal to learn the lesson God is attempting to teach us only delays the inevitability of further life sessions on the same topic until we grasp His Truth. Our embracing of God's lesson redeems the story. My hunch is that Jonah could tell his own story because he survived the Assyrian gourd life session and learned the lesson God was teaching.

What about you? Where are you regarding bitterness? What steps of spiritual recovery is God calling you to take? If you and I are truly followers of the Christ of the cross, we must relinquish each of our perceived rights to His Lordship!

Chapter 9

Walking the Talk

We have traveled a journey that may have exposed the brokenness of your soul. Allow me to expose the brokenness of my own soul and the journey of wholeness and holiness through which God has lovingly led me. I will tell my story through the trajectory which I have used throughout the book: clinging to rights is the trigger that creates expectations, expectations yield frustrations, frustrations lead to appraisals, appraisals spawn anger, and unresolved anger toward those who have wronged us results in bitterness and unforgiveness.

A Story of Healing

Dad and "Uncle" were best friends from their days as students in boarding school. Their friendship endured through college. They raised their children together. My siblings and I called Dad's friend "Uncle." We called Uncle's wife "Aunt." Our families vacationed together. I worked for Uncle in a Christian ministry as a high school and college student.

We were like family.

Uncle was a trustee at their *alma mater*. He was a local pastor. He was a community leader. He was a member of the county school board. I knew him. I loved him. I respected him.

My wife was employed by a neighboring public school district. Uncle's school district and my wife's school district hired new superintendents. Competition was on in earnest. My wife's school district had a history as an academic district. Under the leadership of a new superintendent the district doubled in enrollment. Uncle's school district lost hundreds of students. Open hostility erupted in the local newspapers. Open letters from the superintendents attacking each other and the competing district were weekly occurrences. The pain and bitterness was spreading like a cancer across the community.

One day, Uncle came by my house campaigning for re-election to his school board seat. His visit was at the peak of the community-wide distress. Uncle was accompanied by two political allies. In my driveway, he asked for my vote. I responded that I would support the candidate that best reflected school choice, the main campaign issue.

Uncle responded to his friends. "You can't listen to John. He's biased," was the sentiment I heard. I felt that he spoke down to me, embarrassing me in front of his colleagues. I let him know. I felt attacked, talked down to, and publicly degraded by someone I had loved, trusted, and admired.

That event threw me into a season of temptation and frustration. My emotions and rights were offended, and Uncle was my offender. I felt that I had the right to expect him to protect me and watch out for me. Uncle was the vice president of the umbrella organization where I worked, and my father was the president. I felt that I had the right for him to want me to be part of that organization. My wife's employment was our family's financial support that made my full-time volunteer work within that organization a reality. I wanted Uncle to want me, to value me, and I felt like Uncle was trying to run me off by attacking my wife's job security.

I felt that I had the right to expect him to value me as he would value his own children and seek to protect me and my family. I felt that I had the right to expect him to consider how his political involvement affected our organization and my family. I felt that I had the right to be offended. I had the right to judge his behavior as wrong. I had the right to feel like he was out to get me!

Then my expectations multiplied. I expected Uncle to love me, to care for me, and to consider my interest. I expected Uncle to want me to be a part of his alma mater, and mine, where I was employed. I expected Uncle to act in such a way as to protect that interest. I expected Uncle to treat me with respect in front of his friends. I expected Uncle to put my interest above his elected office. After all we were lifelong friends, and my dad was his best friend.

Frustration flooded my mind. I was frustrated because I felt that our family's livelihood was attacked. I felt rejected and unwanted by Uncle, in his roles as a trustee of my college and as a family friend. I felt betrayed. I felt frustrated that he would not talk to me after the initial encounter in my driveway. I felt frustrated that he seemed to have no empathy, loyalty, or concern for his best friend's son, and the estrangement that he had caused in our relationship.

Then the appraisals came. I tried to assess Uncle's motives. I tried to analyze why he felt so comfortable in embarrassing me in front of his political allies. I began labeling his motives as rejection, arrogance, and spiritual compromise. I construed Uncle as a God-called minister of the Gospel who had allowed political power to go to his head, causing him to lose his way. I judged Uncle as a tragically compromised leader who abandoned the principles upon which he had built his life, for the sake of political expediency. My appraisal went so far as to judge his motives and the state of his eternal soul before God. I had lost confidence in Uncle as a spiritually minded person.

I was angry. I was angry at being rejected, embarrassed, humiliated, unwanted, and passed over. I was angry at my dad's best friend, my Uncle. I was quickly headed down a destructive spiritual path.

In the midst of my personal battle with bitterness and self-destruction, tragedy struck. Uncle was returning to his home from conducting business in the nearby county seat town. He had just concluded the licensing and insuring of a car that had been donated to the ministry he served. A young woman, high on prescription drugs, pulled out directly into Uncle's car. The accident trapped Uncle's broken body inside the car. The life squad had to remove him with the "jaws of life." Uncle was rushed to the local hospital, and then flown by emergency helicopter to the University Medical Center. Dad signed the papers for the life flight.

Uncle was in the fight of his life!

It was a week or so later when I received a phone call. It was Uncle. He started the awkward conversation. He told me that he did not know if he would live or die. He was performing an inventory of his soul. Uncle wanted to know that he was ready to meet the Lord, should his injured body betray him, and he lose his fight for life. He said that only one relationship came to his mind that needed to be repaired before he died. That relationship was with me.

How does one respond to such an overture? I was caught by surprise. In hindsight, I am embarrassed at the direct and emotional way in which I directed my words at Uncle. I am ashamed that I was not more kind and gentle, but I was not. Here is how I recall the charged exchange between us.

Phone in hand, I spoke to Uncle. I vented a belly full of pain and anger at this dying man. My rights, expectations, frustration, appraisals, and anger had festered within me. I had sought God to forgive Uncle throughout the entire affair, but the battle had been hard.

I told Uncle how betrayed, embarrassed, and humiliated I felt by his words toward me. I told him that I expected more from him as a friend and as a spiritual leader. I told him that he was an embarrassment to me and to our entire organization. I let him know that I felt he was trying to run me away from the organization. The pain tumbled out. All of the appraisals and anger were confessed. Although we did not agree on all of the facts, we released our rights. Uncle apologized. I apologized. We forgave each other.

The next day, I told my dad what had happened. Dad told me that he was heading to Lexington that afternoon to visit Uncle. He invited me to join him. I did. We met Uncle at the University Medical Center. His broken body was veiled by a sheet. We read scripture, prayed, and never spoke of our healed wound again. Forgiveness.

Uncle survived that accident, but had to face 18 subsequent surgeries in a quest to repair his broken body. His health was so weakened that Uncle never walked again without assistance. He fought chronic infection. Uncle lived nearly ten more years, until cancer finally took his life.

Before Uncle's funeral, his children called me. They asked me to take part in the service. I led the congregation in singing some of Uncle's favorite hymns. I mourned his passing. I stood at the grave side. We buried Uncle, and I buried a mixture of memories, some painful, others pleasant. My conscience was clear before my God.

A year later, we buried Aunt. Aunt and Uncle's children called me again. They asked me to take part in the service. Again, I led the congregation in singing some of Aunt's favorite hymns. I mourned her passing. I stood at her grave side, healed and whole.

I anticipate seeing Aunt and Uncle in heaven.

Throughout my life, I have enjoyed studying, teaching, and preaching. I have always thrived when I study the Bible, God's Word. Human communication is my second love. My mind is stimulated with studying and teaching healthy communication and relational skills. I have traveled and spoken extensively in evangelism and teaching. Whenever I address the issues of a Biblical response to bitterness, the truth of scripture is guaranteed to hit a raw nerve. I have witnessed various reactions when the raw nerve is irritated.

A Story of Refusal to Heal

One pastor called me late at night after a revival service. I had shared a truth about God's ability to cleanse our hearts from bitterness. This pastor had been through a crushing situation. He felt that he had been falsely accused of an impropriety. A hearing in a local court cleared him. His local church stood beside him, but the denominational hierarchy was not convinced. A church trial convicted him. The pastor refused to accept their judgment, and led a split of a handful of churches from the denomination.

The week of the revival effort had been spent compassionately listening to him and his wife vent their anger at the denomination. They were genuinely hurting. Pastor felt wrongly accused. His wife felt he was wrongly convicted in the church trial. I felt concerned about a spirit of bitterness I sensed throughout the church family. So, I prayed about it. Saturday night, I felt clear to preach a message addressing bitterness.

I did.

People came forward and prayed at the altar.

I retired for the night, exhausted, and prepared for the Sunday morning closing service.

The phone rang.

It was Pastor.

He was hurting, angry, and confused. He had received a call from an offended member of his congregation. Very quickly, the conviction of the service and humble prayers around an altar had turned into defensiveness and self-justification. I was the object of attack now. Pastor accused me of confusing himself and his people. I apologized.

I have never been back to that church.

An Appeal

Bitterness is the secret sin of the Church. We coddle it. We protect it. We insure it. We hide it. We excuse it. We justify it. We even commit the idolatry of selfishly sanctifying our bitterness into a viable virtue! We don't want to confront our bitterness. But the reality is that bitterness is sin. If we don't confront, confess, and seek cleansing from our bitterness, it will destroy us in the here and the hereafter. Bitterness separates us from God. God's nature is love, and our bitterness builds a wall that prevents us from having anything in common with His holy character of perfect love.

Our loving Heavenly Father wants our hearts. He relentlessly pursues us, peeling back the layers of self in an attempt to own our hearts. He demands Lordship!

But self gets in the way. Rights, expectations, frustration, appraisals, and anger have taken their toll on us. Jesus lovingly, tenderly probes the recesses of our consciousness in a quest to know us. He demands surrender. He demands Lordship. He loves us.

If you see yourself in the pages of this book, I appeal to you: embrace a spiritual journey that will take you beyond bitterness. I encourage you to pursue the peace of forgiveness. I urge you to enjoy Christ's assurance of a deep heart cleansing to free you from a disposition inclined toward bitterness, filling you with the Holy Spirit of God, and bestowing God's grace of perfect love upon you. Then, live a life of complete surrender to the Lordship of Jesus Christ, where your rights are abandoned to Him. Keep your finger off the trigger of your rights, and you can live in freedom from the destructive pattern of bitterness.

The same God that loved Jonah through his bitterness loves you. The same God who has loved me through my sorest temptations to bitterness loves you. He wants to walk with you, love you, discipline you, correct you, call you to holiness, and cleanse you from all bitterness.

Made in the USA
Columbia, SC
05 March 2019